FACTS AT YOUR FINGERTIPS

SOUTH AMERICA & OCEANIA

Published by Brown Bear Books Limited

An imprint of
The Brown Reference Group plc
68 Topstone Road
Redding
Connecticut
06896
USA

www.brownreference.com

© 2008 The Brown Reference Group plc

Library of Congress Cataloging-in-Publication Data available
upon request.

ISBN-13 978-1-933834-10-8

Author: Derek Hall
Editorial Director: Lindsey Lowe
Project Director: Graham Bateman
Art Director/Design: Steve McCurdy
Editor: Virginia Carter

Printed in Singapore

Picture credits

Cover Images
Front: Rio de Janeiro, Brazil (Shutterstock/Marcaux)

Back: Uluru, Australia (Shutterstock/Christian McCarty)

Page 1: Mclaren vineyard, Australia (Shutterstock/Ben Goode)

Shutterstock
5 Roux Frederic; 7 Dario Diament; 8 Rafael Martin-Gaitero;
14/15 Mark Van Overmeire;16/17 Galyna Andrushko;
18/19 Marcaux; 21 Salamanderman; 24/25 Olga Gabay;
27 Luis César Tejo; 28/29 Daniela Weinstein; 32/33 Erik
de Graaf Fotografie; 37 Bruce Amos; 39 Christian McCarty;
40 Ximagination; 44/45 Lidian; 48/49 Matthew; 50/51
Thomas Hruschka; 52/53 Hiroshi; 54/55 Pascaline Daniel;
56 Ben Goode; 57 Christophe Testi; 58 Simon Voorwinde;
60/61 Lidian.

TopFoto.co.uk
10/11 © Alinari/TopFoto; 13 Topham
Picturepoint/TopFoto; 34/35 © Alinari/TopFoto; 22
TopFoto/HIP.

Photos.com
30/31; 42/43; 46/47.

CONTENTS

SOUTH AMERICA & OCEANIA

South America is a continent of records. It is home to the world's longest mountain range (the Andes), the driest desert (Atacama), the largest rain forest and largest river by volume (Amazon), the highest waterfall (Angel Falls), the highest railroad (in Peru), the highest capital city (La Paz), the highest commercially navigable lake (Titicaca), and the southernmost town (Puerto Toro). In this volume South America is discussed along with **Oceania**, Indonesia, Australia, New Zealand, and Antartica.

Early Peoples

The native peoples of South America originally migrated south via a land bridge that linked today's Siberia with Alaska. A few of these "early peoples" still exist in Amazonia and have yet to see a "white man." It was once believed that some of the new arrivals, or their successors, went on to inhabit the Pacific islands of Oceania. Most anthropologists now agree, however, that the islands of the Pacific were originally settled from Asia. Some of these islanders migrated from their mythical homeland of Hawaiki in seagoing canoes, to become the ancestors of the Maori people of New Zealand—one of the most recent areas to be settled by humans. Australia's Aboriginal people are also likely to have migrated from Southeast Asia, at least 40,000 years ago, although there is evidence to suggest that they could have come from India or East Africa.

Colonial History

Mainland South America was colonized by Spain and Portugal in the 1500s. The local population was either assimilated, killed, enslaved, or died of "European" diseases, such as smallpox, influenza, and typhus. African slaves were often imported because of their immunity to such diseases.

Some of the first white people to colonize Australia were British convicts, punished by transportation to New South Wales. The coasts of New Zealand and Australia and the islands of the Pacific were explored by seafarers such as Captain James Cook. The latter had claimed New South Wales for Britain in 1770, although the Commonwealth of Australia was not formed until 1901.

Today's South America

Most of mainland South America embraces free-market capitalism, but inflation is a threat in some countries. Like Australia, the whole continent is rich in minerals. Other exports include coffee, cocoa, fruit, meat, and—a cause of great concern—drugs (especially from Colombia). Over the centuries the population has largely become racially integrated, apart from peoples in some remote Andean and Amazonian areas. Spanish, Portuguese, native Indian, and African peoples have intermarried to create a multicultural society. These racial differences will be seen by anyone familiar with Brazil's soccer team. Most people speak Spanish or Portuguese (in Brazil), and the subcontinent is overwhelmingly Roman Catholic.

Natural World

The South American subcontinent comprises the Andes, the tropical rain forest of Amazonia, savanna (or pampas) in Argentina, and the coastal desert of Peru. Wildlife includes anacondas and other snakes, exotic parrots and butterflies, llamas and alpacas, and even, in the extreme south of Chile, penguins.

Much of Australia is either desert or marginal grazing land, but there are tropical forests in the north. In the southeast is the Murray-Darling River system and, adjacent to the coast, the Australian Alps. New Zealand enjoys a temperate climate with a mountain range on the western side of South Island. Australia and New Zealand have wildlife that is found nowhere else on earth—kangaroos and other marsupials in Australia and flightless birds in New Zealand.

The altiplano is a high (3,670-m/12,040-ft), windswept plateau lying between Bolivia's two main Andean mountain ranges—the Cordillera Occidental and the Cordillera Oriental.

COLOMBIA

Situated in the northwest corner of South America, Colombia takes its name from the famous explorer Christopher Columbus (1451–1506). It is a beautiful country with a coastline on both the Pacific Ocean and the Caribbean Sea, separated by the Isthmus of Panama. The country has a rich colonial heritage but is plagued by internal strife and has almost become synonymous with the illegal trafficking in narcotics.

NATIONAL DATA – COLOMBIA

Land area	1,038,700 sq km (401,044 sq mi)			

Climate		Temperatures		Annual
	Altitude m (ft)	January °C(°F)	July °C(°F)	precipitation mm (in)
Bogotá	2,645 (8,678)	11 (55)	11 (55)	799 (31.4)

Major physical features	highest point: Pico Cristóbal Colón 5,800 m (19,029 ft)

Population	(2006 est.) 43,593,035

Form of government	multiparty republic with two legislative houses

Armed forces	army 178,000; navy 22,000; air force 7,000

Largest cities	Bogotá (capital – 7,363, 492); Cali (2,498,074); Medellin (2,042,093); Barranquilla (1,429,031)

Official language	Spanish

Ethnic composition	Mestizo 58%; White 20%; Mulatto 14%; Black 4%; Mixed Black-Amerindian 3%; Amerindian 1%

Religious affiliations	Roman Catholic 90%; other 10%

Currency	1 Colombian peso (COP) = 100 centavos

Gross domestic product	(2006) U.S. $366.7 billion

Gross domestic product per capita	(2006) U.S. $8,400

Life expectancy at birth	male 68.15 yr; female 75.96 yr

Major resources	petroleum, natural gas, coal, iron ore, nickel, gold, copper, , hydropower, bananas, cassava, cattle, coffee, cut flowers, emeralds, maize/corn, platinum, potatoes, rice, silver, sugarcane, sorghum, soybeans, timber

Geography

The mighty Colombian Andes cover about one-third of the land. In the far north, snowcapped Pico Cristóbal Colón forms part of an isolated massif overlooking the Caribbean to the north and a swampy basin to the east. Two main rivers, the Magdalena and the Cauca, flow into the basin through deep trenches separating the three main ranges of the Andes: the Cordillera Occidental, overlooking the Pacific coastal plain, the volcanic Cordillera Central east of the Cauca River, and the Cordillera Oriental, farther east still, beyond the Magdalena valley. Earthquakes and eruptions show that the region is geologically active.

More than half the country consists of a sparsely populated plain that drops southeast from the Andes toward Peru and Brazil. The northern lowlands are drained by the Orinoco River, running along the border with Venezuela. The southern lowlands form part of the Amazon Basin. It is relatively dry in the Caribbean lowlands, but the Pacific coast, central valleys, and Amazonian lowlands have tropical rain forest with higher rainfall, giving way to savanna in the northern lowlands and valleys. Humans have stripped away most of the original forest, but the moist mountain forests still support animals such as tapirs, sloths, anteaters, howler monkeys, jaguars, and hummingbirds. Caimans and capybaras are found in the rivers.

Society

In the 16th century Spanish invaders overcame the indigenous Chibcha peoples—craftsmen highly skilled at working gold and jewelry. The colonists founded the city of Bogotá, and Colombia became the heart of the Viceroyalty of New Granada. Its independence was gained in 1819, however, and until 1830 it was part of the Republic of Gran Colombia, which included Ecuador, Venezuela, and Panama. Modern Colombia's history is one of unrest, beginning with a revolt in 1840 and the emergence of opposing liberal and conservative political factions. Multiparty elections since 1974 have brought little peace; guerrilla groups and paramilitaries have grown in strength since the 1990s and have caused large-scale violence and civilian death, much of it fueled by illegal drug trafficking and extortion.

Economy

The economy, founded mainly on private enterprise, is based on agriculture, but it is becoming increasingly industrialized. Only a small part of the land is cultivated, but the crops are vital to the economy. They include bananas and cassava in the lowlands, and maize/corn and potatoes in the mountains. Coffee accounts for one-third of all official export revenue, but cannabis and coca—from which the drug cocaine is produced—provide the drug cartels with twice this amount. Colombia has the largest coal reserves in Latin America. It also has huge natural gas reserves, and produces 60 percent of the world's emeralds. In the late 1990s the government began to privatize coal, oil, and electricity production, but guerrilla activity hampered investment by foreign companies. Coffee and food processing are important industries, as are chemicals and automobiles.

Colombia's impressive architecture, such as this building in the capital, Bogotá, is a legacy from colonial days.

COLOMBIA'S DIVERSE ETHNIC MIX

Colombia's colonial past is also reflected in today's population, many of whom are of mixed ancestry. Most of these are mestizos (people of European and Amerindian descent), but mulattos (people of mixed African and European origin) form the majority along the coast. There is a large white minority in the country, and small numbers of blacks and Amerindians, the latter divided into as many as 400 different groups. Although Spanish is the country's official language, many other languages are also spoken. The vast majority of the population is Roman Catholic.

VENEZUELA

Once a poor country, Venezuela's economy was radically transformed by the discovery of vast petroleum reserves. However, huge inequalities of wealth exist, and 67 percent of the population lives below the poverty line.

Geography

Venezuela's diverse and dramatic scenery is crowned by the Angel Falls, the highest waterfall in the world that cascades down 979 m (3,212 ft) on the Carrao River.

Northwestern Venezuela is shaped by two northern arms of the Andes. The western branch, the Sierra de Perijá, defines part of the Colombian border. The eastern branch, the Cordillera de Mérida, includes the country's highest peak, Pico Bolívar. Between the two ranges lie the swampy Maracaibo Lowlands surrounding huge Lake Maracaibo, an extension of the Gulf of Venezuela. Further mountain ranges run eastward along the coast,

Abutting the northern edge of Caracas, the El Ávila National Park acts as a natural barrier between the capital and the coast.

NATIONAL DATA – VENEZUELA

Land area	882,050 sq km (340,561 sq mi)			

Climate		Temperatures		Annual
	Altitude m (ft)	January °C(°F)	July °C(°F)	precipitation mm (in)
Caracas	1,042 (3,419)	26 (79)	24 (75)	914 (35.9)

Major physical features highest point: Pico Bolívar 5,007 m (16,427 ft); longest river: Orinoco 2,061 km (1,281 mi)

Population (2006 est.) 25,730,435

Form of government federal multiparty republic with two legislative houses

Armed forces army 34,000; navy 18,300; air force 7,000

Largest cities Caracas (capital – 1,801,562); Maracaibo (2,054,039); Valencia (1,457,912); Barquisimeto (833,338); Ciudad Guayana (792,508); Maracay (399,446); Petare (386,712); Barcelona (459,148); Maturin (445,451); Turmero (373,871)

Official language Spanish

Ethnic composition Mestizo 69%; White 20%; Black 9%; Amerindian 2%

Religious affiliations Roman Catholic 96%; Protestant 2%; other 2%

Currency 1 bolivar (VEB) = 100 centimos

Gross domestic product (2006) U.S. $176.4 billion

Gross domestic product per capita (2006) U.S. $6,900

Life expectancy at birth male 71.49 yr; female 77.81 yr

Major resources petroleum, natural gas, iron ore, gold, bauxite, manganese, other minerals, hydropower, diamonds, bananas, coal, cocoa, coffee, livestock, maize/corn, rice, sorghum, sugarcane, tobacco, vegetables

sheltering several cities, including the capital, Caracas. South of the mountains are the lowland plains of the Orinoco Basin, which cross the country from Colombia to near the Guyanan border. Farther south is the huge, irregular granite plateau of the Guiana Highlands, where the Orinoco rises.

The climate is mainly tropical, with a rainy season. However, highland areas are cooler with variable rainfall. The driest areas are in the lee of mountains; the Orinoco Basin receives the highest rainfall, whereas the plains are flooded in the rainy season but otherwise mostly arid. Forests still cover much of the country, ranging from evergreen in northern mountains to tropical rain forest around the Orinoco Delta and far south. Wild, mainly uninhabited grassland covers most of the rest of the land. Animals, restricted to remote areas by the spread of humans, include bears, caimans, ocelots, peccaries, and opossums. Manatees and dolphins are found in coastal regions. To protect the wildlife, hunting is forbidden to all except Amerindians, who depend on it for their way of life.

Society

Various Amerindian peoples were living in the area when Spaniards formed the first European settlement in 1523. Until the beginning of the 19th century Venezuela was in the hands of Spanish administrators and priests. It was in Venezuela that Francisco Miranda (1750–1816) and Simón Bolívar (1783–1830) began South America's struggle for independence. After the final defeat of the Spanish in 1821, Venezuela, Ecuador, and Colombia briefly united to form the Republic of Gran Colombia. Venezuela left the union in 1829 and was ruled by military dictators for more than a century.

In the 1920s the establishment of a major petroleum industry initiated an era of greater prosperity and growth. Lasting democratic government followed in 1959. The current government under Hugo Chavez (b. 1954) has introduced free healthcare, subsidised food, and land reforms, but critics accuse him of being authoritarian. Primary education is free and compulsory. Welfare is well developed, although the drift to urban centers has resulted in shanty towns springing up. There has also been a buildup of drug-related problems and

VENEZUELAN PETROLEUM INDUSTRY

The petroleum industry is the mainstay of the economy, accounting for about one-third of GDP, some 80 percent of export earnings, and nearly three-quarters of government revenue. The country's largest oil fields are located in Lake Maracaibo, a shallow inland sea on the northwest coast. The United States is an major importer of Venezuelan petroleum. However, such a dependence on one resource can have damaging consequences. For example, in the late 1990s sharply fluctuating oil prices caused the government to adopt austerity measures and hampered efforts to modernize the economy.

irresponsible mining operations that are endangering the rain forest and the indigenous peoples. Most of the population are mestizos of mixed European and Amerindian origin, but there are substantial white and black minorities. Few pure Amerindians remain.

Economy

Petroleum and natural resources account for the majority of the country's export income. Petroleum, natural gas, and hydroelectricity enable Venezuela to be self-sufficient in meeting industrial and domestic power needs. The petrochemical industry is centered mainly on Morón to the west of Caracas and near the Gulf of Venezuela and Lake Maracaibo. The city of Maracaibo produces food, pharmaceuticals, machinery, and electrical equipment. Local iron ores are processed in the east, and significant amounts of gold and diamonds are also extracted.

Only a small proportion of the land is used for agriculture and, despite agrarian reforms, modernization programs, and extensive irrigation of the lowland plains, some food is still imported. The chief crops include bananas, sorghum, and maize/corn, while cash crops include coffee, sugarcane, and tobacco. Cattle are the most important livestock, grazed especially on the lowland plains. Fishing has great potential but is not fully exploited, although anchovies, sardines, and shellfish are caught by coastal fleets. The roads are best developed in the north, with three major highways.

GUYANA

Formerly known as British Guiana, the small state of Guyana has a diverse landscape including forested plateaus, savanna grassland, coastline, and numerous rivers. The country's name is derived from the Amerindian word meaning "land of the waters."

Geography

Guyana's narrow coastal plain is mostly land reclaimed from the sea and protected by dikes and crisscrossed by

NATIONAL DATA – GUYANA

Land area	196,850 sq km (76,004 sq mi)			

Climate		Temperatures		Annual
	Altitude m (ft)	January °C(°F)	July °C(°F)	precipitation mm (in)
Georgetown	2 (7)	26 (79)	27 (80)	2,160 (85)

Major physical features highest point: Roraima 2,810m (9,219 ft); longest river: Essequibo 1,014 km (630 mi)

Population (2006 est.) 767,245

Form of government multiparty republic with one legislative house

Armed forces army 900; navy 100; air force 100

Capital city Georgetown (238,747)

Official language English

Ethnic composition East Indian 50%; Black 36%; Amerindian 7%; White, Chinese, and mixed 7%

Religious affiliations Christian 50%; Hindu 35%; Muslim 10%; other 5%

Currency 1 Guyanese dollar (GYD) = 100 cents

Gross domestic product (2006) U.S. $3.62 billion

Gross domestic product per capita (2006) U.S. $4,700

Life expectancy at birth male 63.21 yr; female 68.65 yr

Major resources bauxite, gold, diamonds, hardwood timber, shrimp, fish, coconuts, oranges, rice, semiprecious gems, sugarcane

canals. Most of the country, however, consists of an irregular, thickly forested plateau. Straddling the western border are the ancient Pakaraima Mountains—including Mount Roraima, the country's highest peak and inspiration for the novel *The Lost World* by British writer Sir Arthur Conan Doyle (1859–1930). The Rupununi area in the southwest of the country supports savanna grassland interspersed by low mountain ranges.

Guyana's forests consist mainly of tropical hardwoods. The country is rich in wildlife, including manatees and capybaras in and beside the rivers, sloths and jaguars in the forests, and giant anteaters and armadillos on the savanna. The varied birdlife includes toucans and brilliantly plumaged hummingbirds.

Road and rail links are scarce in Guyana, so traveling by boat along the many rivers is one of the best ways to get around.

Guyana's climate is hot and frequently humid, with heavy seasonal rainfalls bringing flooding to the poorly drained soils.

Society

Arawaks and Caribs were the original inhabitants of the region before European settlers came. The first to arrive were the Dutch, who brought thousands of slaves to work on the sugarcane plantations. The British then occupied the area around the Demerara River, and by 1814 had secured most of modern-day Guyana. After the abolition of slavery, immigrant workers were imported from Asia. In 1923 British Guiana became a crown colony, and by 1966 it had achieved full independence as Guyana. The country became a republic in 1970 under Prime Minister Forbes Burnham (1923–85), who became executive president in 1980. In 1992, what is considered to be the country's first truly free and fair election since independence was held.

Economy

Guyana has a mixed economy that saw steady growth in the late 1990s caused by expansion of agriculture and mining. Although agriculture is an important industry, it is more or less confined to the coastal region, where the majority of the people works. Plantation sugarcane is the main crop, followed by rice and coconuts. Some livestock rearing is also undertaken, mainly in the Rupununi valley in the southwest.

Guyana's industrial base is dominated by its world-class deposits of bauxite, which form the main export commodity. The principal imports are fuel and manufactured goods. There is potential to develop hydroelectricity as a source of power but, like the country's timber and other mineral reserves, it has not been fully exploited. Poor road and rail links in all but the coastal areas hamper development, and light aircraft provide vital links between coastal and inland communities. Health and welfare schemes are adequate, but poor housing remains a problem. Good education is generally available, and literacy levels are high.

THE PEOPLE OF GUYANA

Guyanans are remarkable for their racial diversity. The great majority of the population is descended from Asian Indians or Africans. Amerindians are a minority here, but make up the dominant group in the villages of the sparsely populated interior. The country also has small Chinese and European communities. Religion and language reflect the cultural mix. The main language is English (Guyana is the only country in South America where English is the official language), but creole and Hindi are also spoken. Most people are Christian, but there are also Hindus and Muslims.

Formerly known as Dutch Guiana, Suriname is a small republic on the north-central coast of South America that gained independence in 1975. It is a nation of mixed cultures.

Geography

The landscape divides into three broad areas. The coastal plain is a low, narrow, swampy region consisting chiefly of artificially drained or reclaimed land. The soil here is rich and fertile, and this where most of the population is found. Farther inland, the terrain rises to a low savanna plateau. In the south the plateau becomes higher and more rugged as it rises toward the Guiana Highlands, with low mountains and thick forests. Several rivers rise near the border with Brazil and flow northward; the Courantyne River forms the border with Guyana, while the Maroni and Litani Rivers straddle the border with French Guiana. The climate is hot and very humid, moderated only by light sea breezes, and there is heavy seasonal rainfall. The forests inland consist mainly of tropical hardwoods, but there are mangroves along the coast. Suriname's wildlife is plentiful and varied. The forested regions support tapirs, sloths, ocelots, jaguars, snakes, bats, colorful birds such as parrots, and many different kinds of insects and spiders.

Society

The Surinen peoples, for whom the country is named, had for the most part been ousted by other indigenous tribes before European colonists arrived. The Dutch secured the colony from Britain in 1667, in exchange for New Amsterdam (later New York). From 1682 the Dutch West India Company imported African slaves to work its tea and coffee plantations. Many of them escaped into the interior, where their descendants are known as "bush blacks." After the abolition of slavery in 1863, laborers were brought in from India, China, and Java to work the land.

Suriname gained full independence in 1975, but racial conflicts led to a coup in 1980 under Lieutenant-

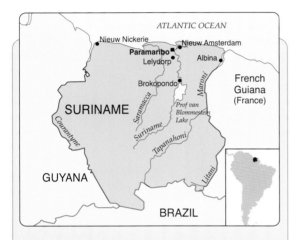

NATIONAL DATA – SURINAME

Land area	161,470 sq km (62,344 sq mi)			

Climate		Temperatures		Annual
	Altitude m (ft)	January °C(°F)	July °C(°F)	precipitation mm (in)
Paramaribo	4 (13)	26 (79)	27 (80)	2,312 (91)

Major physical features	highest point: Juliana Top 1,230 m (4,035 ft)

Population	(2006 est.) 439,117

Form of government	multiparty republic with one legislative house

Armed forces	army 1,400; navy 240; air force 200

Capital city	Paramaribo (226,124)

Official language	Dutch

Ethnic composition	Hindustani 37%; Creole 31%; Javanese 15%; "Maroons" 10%; Amerindian 2%; Chinese 2%; white 1%; other 2%

Religious affiliations	Hindu 27.4%; Protestant 25.2% (mainly Moravian); Roman Catholic 22.8%; Muslim 19.6%; traditional beliefs 5%

Currency	1 Surinam dollar (SRD) = 100 cents

Gross domestic product	(2006) U.S. $3.098 billion

Gross domestic product per capita	(2006) U.S. $7,100

Life expectancy at birth	male 66.66 yr; female 71.47 yr

Major resources	timber, hydropower, fish, kaolin, shrimp, bauxite, gold, nickel, copper, platinum, iron ore, bananas, cattle, citrus fruits, cocoa, coconuts, coffee, rice, sugarcane

THE PEOPLES OF SURINAME

Bush blacks make up the majority of the population of the interior, and the spread of their settlements has nudged the Amerindian minority deeper into the jungle, although the two groups coexist in harmony. The main ethnic groups are the Asian Indians, which make up 37 percent of the population, and the Creole (people of mixed descent). There are also significant populations of Javanese and Chinese. Suriname's official language is Dutch, but many other languages are also spoken, including a lingua franca known as Sranan. The major religions are Christianity, Hinduism, and Islam.

Suriname village life. Most of the population lives in the fertile coastal area, where much of the land has been reclaimed from the sea.

Colonel Dési Bouterse (b. 1945). Foreign aid was withdrawn, the economy collapsed, and the Jungle Commandos—a bush blacks organization—began a guerrilla campaign that threatened to destabilize the country. Bouterse lost the 1988 election. The new civilian government formed a peace pact with the Jungle Commandos, but Bouterse staged another coup in 1990. A peace accord was signed in 1992, and elections were held in 1996. In 2000, following public dissent over rampant inflation, elections brought in the New Front for Democracy and Development, a coalition which again won the elections held in 2005.

Economy

Suriname's economic potential is high, although it relies heavily on foreign aid from the Netherlands. Agriculture is mainly confined to the fertile coastal plain, and less than 10 percent of the workforce is engaged in farming. The main crop is rice, some of which is exported. Other crops include sugarcane and bananas. The rearing of livestock is only small-scale, but forestry and fishing satisfy domestic needs with enough surplus for export. Most of the country's exports are provided by its rich bauxite deposits—they account for more than one-third of GDP. The bauxite is smelted to aluminum using local hydroelectric power.

Roads are mainly confined to coastal areas, and transportation elsewhere is largely by water or air.

ECUADOR

As its name suggests, Ecuador lies astride the equator on the west coast of South America. It also includes the Galápagos Islands about 1,000 km (600 mi) to the west in the Pacific Ocean.

Geography

The terrain of mainland Ecuador is characterized by high mountains and a tendency to suffer earthquakes and landslides. The coastal lowlands are mainly fertile alluvial plains dotted with volcanic hills. Most industry and commerce is located in this region. Inland, the huge bulk of the Andes Mountains crosses the country from north to south. It forms two parallel chains intersected by high valleys with river basins, one of which is the site of Quito, the capital. At 2,850 m (9,350 ft) Quito is the world's second highest capital city after La Paz in Bolivia. Many of the highest peaks are volcanic, including Cotopaxi in the north of the country. On the eastern slopes of the Andes the land drops into the impenetrable rain forest of the Amazon Basin. Here, in this little-known region, the exact borders with neighboring Peru are disputed.

Ecuador's climate is generally hot and humid, particularly in the east, although in the mountains temperatures are much colder. The coastal region is cooled by the Humboldt Current, which also reduces rainfall on parts of the coast.

At 5,911 m (19,388 ft), Cotopaxi in the Ecuadorean Andes is the world's highest active volcano. It has erupted 50 times since 1738.

NATIONAL DATA – ECUADOR

Land area	276,840 sq km (106,889 sq mi)

Climate	Altitude m (ft)	Temperatures January °C(°F)	July °C(°F)	Annual precipitation mm (in)
Quito	2,879 (9,446)	15 (59)	15 (59)	1,116 (43.9)

Major physical features highest point: Chimborazo 6,267 m (20,561 ft); longest river: Napo (part) 1,100 km (700 mi)

Population (2006 est.) 13,547,510

Form of government multiparty republic with one legislative house

Armed forces army 37,500; navy 5,500; air force 4,000

Largest cities Guayaquil (1,952,029); Quito (capital – 1,399,814); Cuenca (276,974); Machala (198,123); Santo Domingo de los Colorados (200,421)

Official language Spanish

Ethnic composition Mestizo (mixed Amerindian and White) 65%; Amerindian 25%; Spanish and others 7%; Black 3%

Religious affiliations Roman Catholic 95%; other 5%

Currency 1 U.S. dollar (USD) = 100 cents

Gross domestic product (2006) U.S. $60.48 billion

Gross domestic product per capita (2006) U.S. $4,500

Life expectancy at birth male 73.55 yr; female 79.43 yr

Major resources petroleum, fish, timber, hydropower, bananas, cassava, cacao, coffee, natural gas, gold, limestone, livestock, maize/corn, oranges, potatoes, rice, sugarcane

Society

During the 15th century an Amerindian kingdom on the mainland was conquered by the Incas, the dominant peoples from Peru. The Inca empire was later weakened by civil war, and it was quickly overrun by Spanish conquistadors in the 1530s. Spanish settlers divided the country into large estates worked by Amerindian laborers. This situation remained unchanged until independence movements grew up among the middle classes in the 19th century.

In 1830, after two decades of war, Ecuador gained independence. A divide between the conservative landowners of Quito and the liberal commercial classes around Guayaquil (sentiments that survive in modern-day Ecuador) resulted in a series of ruthless dictatorships running the country until World War II, when Ecuador lost some territory to Peru. The postwar period was dominated by President José María Velasco Ibarra

THE UNIQUE GALÁPAGOS ISLANDS

The Galápagos are an archipelago formed by the cones of young volcanoes. Their shores consist of arid lava rocks, and only the peaks are forested. Kept cool and dry by the Humboldt Current around their shores, the islands have a unique wildlife which includes marine iguanas that feed on submerged seaweed, giant tortoises, flightless cormorants, and 13 species of Darwin's Finch, named after naturalist Charles Darwin (1809–82). He was inspired to propound his theories of evolution after studying their diversity. The islands are protected for research but have a limited tourist trade.

(1893–1979), whose policies often hampered economic development. Military rule in the 1970s preceded a series of more liberal civilian presidents. In 1995 a short, inconclusive border war was fought with Peru. The 1976 constitution provides for a four-year presidential term, but as recently as 2000 there was yet another short-lived coup before civilian government was restored.

Economy

Ecuador's economy is based largely on agriculture. Bananas are the chief cash crop, along with sugarcane, coffee, and cacao. Rice and potatoes form the main staples. Most food is grown on huge hacienda estates, despite land reforms. Livestock is reared along the coast and in the mountain valleys. Ecuador's great hardwood forests remain largely unexploited, but the country's fishing industry is one of the largest in South America.

Petroleum and natural gas are the main resources and form the chief exports, but sharp fluctuations in oil prices mean that they are vulnerable commodities. In the late 1990s natural disasters coupled with falling oil prices seriously affected the economy and worsened the levels of poverty. The country remains poor, with 70 percent of the population below the poverty line. Transportation is hindered by the terrain; road and rail networks are limited, and mules are often the most effective means of land transportation. Social welfare schemes exist, but healthcare and living conditions are often poor, especially in rural areas.

PERU

Peru derives its name from a Quechua word implying abundance, recalling the former opulence of the Inca and Spanish empires. However, the country's modern development has been hindered in part by the hostile, though often spectacular, terrain. There are also huge inequalities, with an elite ethnic Spanish population controlling most of the country's wealth.

NATIONAL DATA – PERU

Land area	1,280,000 sq km (494,210 sq mi)			

Climate		Temperatures		Annual precipitation
	Altitude m (ft)	January °C(°F)	July °C(°F)	mm (in)
Lima	120 (394)	22 (77)	17 (81)	13 (0.5)

Major physical features	highest point: Huascarán 6,768 m (22,205 ft)

Population	(2006 est.) 28,302,603

Form of government	multiparty republic

Armed forces	army 40,000; navy 25,000; air force 15,000

Largest cities Lima (capital – 7,979,965); Arequipa (878,129); Trujillo (788,911); Chiclayo (607,121); Iquitos (468,687)

Official languages Spanish, Quechua

Ethnic composition Amerindian 45%; Mestizo (mixed Amerindian and White) 37%; White 15%; Black, Japanese, Chinese, and other 3%

Religious affiliations Roman Catholic 81%; Seventh Day Adventist 1.4%; other Christian 0.7%; other 0.6%; unspecified or none 16.3%

Currency	1 nuevo sol (PEN) = 100 centimos

Gross domestic product	(2006) U.S. $181.8 billion

Gross domestic product per capita	(2006) U.S. $6,400

Life expectancy at birth	male 68.05 yr; female 71.71 yr

Major resources copper, silver, gold, petroleum, timber, fish, iron ore, coal, phosphate, potash, hydropower, natural gas, cattle, cotton, fruit, lead, livestock, potatoes, rice, sugarcane, tungsten, uranium, vegetables, wheat, zinc

Geography

Peru is divided into three geographical regions from west to east. The narrow coastal plain runs the length of the Pacific coast. Large parts are arid desert, caused by the Peruvian, or Humboldt, Current cooling the air and preventing rain. However, the Andean rivers have laid down areas of alluvial soils. Most of the population lives in these fertile plains. The Andes create a continuous backbone that enters from Ecuador and broadens at the border with Chile and Bolivia. The mountains are at their most dramatic in central Peru. In the south is an extensive high plateau, the Altiplano, at whose center is Lake Titicaca. The Andes fall away northeast to the Montaña—the deep forested valleys that lead into the rain forests of the Amazon Basin. This wild region is almost uninhabited. The whole country is liable to earthquakes, and several volcanoes in the south are merely dormant. The Amazon Basin's climate is hot and humid, but the mountains are much colder

Machu Picchu, set high up on the eastern flank of the Peruvian Andes, was once a religious center for the Inca empire.

governments alternating with military juntas, guerrilla activity, drug trafficking, and corruption. Peru's instability is partly a result of the ethnic and social divisions between the Spanish-speaking mestizos of the coastal region and the Quechua-speaking Amerindians of the Andes.

Economy

Peru is rich in minerals and other resources, and the economy is heavily dependent on their export. Agriculture, which occupies less than 10 percent of the workforce, is limited by the lack of arable land, most of which is near the coast and requires irrigation to grow crops such as rice and sugarcane. Highland farming is mostly at the subsistence level. Crops here include wheat, potatoes, and coca—which supplies the illegal cocaine trade. Sheep, llamas, and alpacas are reared, mainly for their wool. The fishing fleet is large, but fortunes fluctuate as a result of El Niño.

Industry is powered mainly by hydroelectricity. Copper ore is the major mineral resource, but petroleum is growing in importance. Uranium, iron, and silver are among other mineral exports. Manufacturing industries are concentrated around the capital, Lima, and at Callao, the main port. Poverty and unemployment remain high, and housing, health conditions, and education are generally inadequate in many areas. Transportation is limited by the difficult terrain and climate, and there are few railroads.

with rain and snow. An occasional switch from cold to warm sea currents produces the El Niño phenomenon, causing flooding and a reduction of marine plankton, leading to a loss of coastal fish. Wildlife is varied, ranging from plants that include hardwoods and cacti to animals such as condors, vicuñas, and pelicans.

Society

Ancient Peru was the center for several Amerindian cultures, notably the Chavín, the Nasca, and the Huari. In the 15th century the Incas took over the whole country, building massive cities and roads, until they were defeated by Spanish conquistadors. Peru remained a Spanish treasurehouse until its liberation by Argentine general José de San Martin (1778–1850) in 1821. Peru's recent political history has seen a succession of civilian

RISE AND FALL OF THE INCA EMPIRE

According to legend, the first Inca ruler came to power in South America in 1200. What is known for certain is that after about 1440 the Inca empire stretched for thousands of kilometers from Colombia to Chile, and included large parts of Bolivia and Argentina. The Inca built many roads and massive stone cities, and located their capital at Cuzco. Their religion was based on sun worship and often involved elaborate ceremonies and animal sacrifices. Their downfall came in 1532, when they were conquered by an invading Spanish army led by adventurer Francisco Pizarro (c.1475–1541).

BRAZIL

The largest country in South America and the fifth largest in the world, Brazil has a 7,400-km (4,600-mi) coastline and shares borders with many other countries.

Land area 8,456,510 sq km (3,265,077 sq mi)

Climate	Altitude m (ft)	Temperatures January °C(°F)	July °C(°F)	Annual precipitation mm (in)
Manaus	83 (272)	27 (81)	27 (81)	2,386 (93.9)
Brasilia	1,006 (3,301)	22 (72)	19 (66)	1,632 (64.2)
Rio de Janeiro	61 (200)	27 (81)	22 (72)	1,173 (46.1)

Major physical features highest point: Pico de Neblina 3,014 m (9,889 ft); longest river: Amazon (part) 6,436 km (4,000 mi)

Population (2006 est.) 188,078,227

Form of government federal multiparty republic with two legislative houses

Armed forces army 189,000; navy 32,850; air force 65,309

Largest cities Sao Paulo (10,095,244); Rio de Janeiro (6,086,917); Salvador (2,810,334); Belo Horizonte (2,424,579); Fortaleza (2,390,058); Brasilia (capital – 2,314,172); Curitiba (1,776,074); Manaus (1,690,331); Recife (1,500,293); Belem (1,465,670)

Official language Portuguese

Ethnic composition White 53.7%; Mulatto (mixed White and Black) 38.5%; Black 6.2%; other (includes Japanese, Arab, Amerindian) 0.9%; unspecified 0.7%

Religious affiliations Roman Catholic 73.6%; Protestant 15.4%; Spiritualist 1.3%; Bantu/voodoo 0.3%; other 1.8%; unspecified 0.2%; none 7.4%

Currency 1 real (BRL) = 100 centavos

Gross domestic product (2006) U.S. $1.616 trillion

Gross domestic product per capita (2006) U.S. $8,600

Life expectancy at birth male 68.02 yr; female 76.12 yr

Major resources bauxite, gold, iron ore, manganese, nickel, phosphates, platinum, tin, uranium, petroleum, hydropower, timber, asbestos, bananas, beryllium, cassava, cereals, chromium, coffee, coal, cocoa, cotton, crude oil, diamonds, fish, graphite, livestock, natural gas, oranges, quartz crystal, rice, rubber, salt, silver, soybeans, sugarcane, titanium, tobacco, tourism, tungsten, zinc

It has attracted settlers from all over the world, but its development as a modern industrial state has been overshadowed by problems of inadequate finance, overpopulation, and environmental damage.

Geography

Brazil's northern frontier runs through the mountains and plateaus of the Guiana Highlands, which include Pico da Neblina, the country's highest point. The generally low-lying Amazon Basin immediately to the south covers most of the north of the country and contains the world's largest river system (with more than 1,000 tributaries) as well as lakes, swamps, flood plains, and a coastal delta. The Brazilian Highlands, rising from the Amazon Basin, cover most of the rest of the country and are the most populated region. They consist mainly of broad tablelands cut by deep river valleys. Rio de Janeiro and São Paulo, the two largest cities, nestle in these highlands. In the west, bordering Bolivia and Paraguay, the swampy lowland plains of the Pantanal form the northernmost extension of the Gran Chaco.

THE BRAZILIAN RAIN FORESTS

Much of Brazil is forested; the tropical rain forests of the Amazon Basin have more diversity of plant species than any other habitat on Earth. The animal life in the Amazon Basin is as varied and numerous as the plant life. Many different species of monkeys, reptiles, birds, amphibians, insects, and spiders are found in the trees, and the rivers teem with caimans, capybaras, river dolphins, and as many as 1,500 known species of fish. However, this vast and vital habitat—and the lives of the indigenous peoples— is threatened by its ongoing destruction to make way for cattle ranching and mining.

Society

From its early colonial Portuguese origins Brazil has created a remarkably integrated society, united in part by a language (Portuguese) and a religion (Roman Catholicism) adopted by many people. Just over half the population is of European descent, but most of the rest are mixed European, African, and Amerindian.

Economy

The country has vast natural resources but lacks the capital to exploit them effectively. Successive governments have struggled with foreign debt and massive inflation. The situation became critical in the late 1990s, but the economy later bounced back. Nevertheless severe inequalities of wealth exist, and the northeast in particular remains underdeveloped. Most of the arable land is along the coast and in the south.

Brazil is self-sufficient in food and exports the surplus, with soybeans, sugarcane, and coffee (of which Brazil is the world's second largest producer) the main export crops. Most livestock rearing is in the south, which is also the center for the meat-packing industry. Lumber is generally used for fuel, but large hydroelectric projects now provide power for industrial development. Brazil has rich mineral resources and an expanding and varied industrial sector including petroleum refining and chemicals. Service industries include tourism.

The sprawling city of Rio de Janeiro was, until 1960, the national capital of Brazil. Rio stands at the entrance to Guanabara Bay.

BOLIVIA

Bolivia, a large landlocked state in central South America, is named for independence fighter Simón Bolívar (1783–1830). Since it broke from Spanish rule in 1825 its political history has been punctuated by nearly 200 coups and countercoups. Although Bolivia's natural resources are plentiful, it is the most indebted nation in South America and there is widespread social unrest.

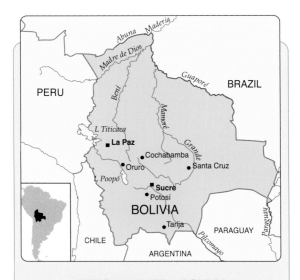

NATIONAL DATA – BOLIVIA

Land area	1,084,390 sq km (418,685 sq mi)			

Climate		Temperatures		Annual
	Altitude m (ft)	January °C(°F)	July °C(°F)	precipitation mm (in)
La Paz	4,103 (13,461)	12 (72)	9 (82)	571 (22.4)

Major physical features highest point: Sajama 6,520 m (21,391 ft); largest lake: Lake Titicaca (part) 3,810 sq km (3,200 sq mi)

Population (2006 est.) 8,989,046

Form of government multiparty republic with two legislative houses

Armed forces army 25,000; navy 5,000; air force 3,000

Largest cities Santa Cruz (1,468,658); Cochabamba (966,049); El Alto (911,525); La Paz (administrative capital - 820, 888); Sucre (judicial capital - 240,604); Oruro (211,217)

Official languages Spanish, Quechua, Aymará

Ethnic composition Quechua 30%; Mestizo (mixed White and Amerindian) 30%; Aymará 25%; White 15%

Religious affiliations Roman Catholic 95%; Protestant (Evangelical Methodist) 5%

Currency 1 boliviano (BOB) = 100 centavos

Gross domestic product (2006) U.S. $27.21 billion

Gross domestic product per capita (2006) U.S. $3,000

Life expectancy at birth male 63.21 yr; female 68.61 yr

Major resources tin, natural gas, petroleum, zinc, tungsten, antimony, silver, iron, lead, gold, timber, hydropower, alpacas, barley, bismuth, cassava, cocoa, coffee, copper, cotton, fruits, llamas, maize/corn, potatoes, quinol, rice, sheep, sugar beet, sugarcane, sulfur, tobacco

Geography

Most of Bolivia's population is concentrated in the west on the Altiplano, a 3,700-m (12,000-ft) high plateau between two lofty ranges of the Andes Mountains. The Cordillera Occidental on the Chilean frontier includes several active volcanoes. The Cordillera Oriental in the east is covered with thick forest. At the northernmost end of the Altiplano is Lake Titicaca, which extends into Peru. La Paz lies to the southeast of Lake Titicaca and is the world's highest capital. Although the Altiplano is the most densely populated part of Bolivia, it is still largely a vast emptiness of coarse grasses and scrub, grazed by vicuñas, llamas, and alpacas and with the air scoured by soaring condors. The southern part of the Altiplano is an arid tableland scattered with salt flats. The Cordillera Occidental descends sharply to the northeast through the cliffs and cloud forests of the Yungas to the vast lowlands of the Oriente, occupying the north and east. Bolivia lies in the tropics, but local climate varies greatly. Seasonal rains are high in the rain forests of the northern Oriente, moderate near Lake Titicaca, and very sparse in the south.

Society

In the 7th century A.D. the area to the south of Lake Titicaca was the center of the first great Andean empire—that of the Aymará people. It survived despite the arrival of the Incas in the 13th century and the Spanish in the 16th century. In 1809 uprisings in La Paz and elsewhere signaled the beginning of South America's struggle for independence. In 1824 rebel leader José de Sucre (1783–1830), a lieutenant of revolutionary commander Simón Bolívar, routed the Spanish at Ayacucho in Peru, bringing independence the following year. Disputes with Chile led in 1879 to the War of the Pacific and resulted in Bolivia losing its only outlet to the sea. A series of bloody internal struggles and military coups began in 1943, but democratic rule was established in 1982. Since then leaders have faced problems caused by deep-rooted poverty, social unrest, and illegal drug trading.

Bolivia's ethnic and cultural mix is a complex one. The largest group is the mestizos of mixed Spanish and Amerindian ancestry mainly in the west, but they are

The distinctive Arbol de Piedra, or stone tree—one of the several strangely shaped, wind-carved rock formations on the Altiplano.

outnumbered by the Amerindian Quechua and Aymará together, many of whom live in the eastern lowlands.

Economy

Almost half the labor force works on the land, many as subsistence farmers. Coffee and sugar are the main exports, although coca fuels a massive illegal drug trade. On the Altiplano herdsman rear their livestock of sheep and other hardy animals on the meager grazing. Bolivia has considerable mineral resources, notably tin, tungsten, zinc, and antimony, although natural gas is the chief legal export. Petroleum production is sufficient to meet local needs. Most of the country's electricity comes from hydroelectric plants.

Roads are confined mainly to the Altiplano, and few are surfaced. Railroad links with Peru and Chile carry Andean minerals to Pacific ports.

AGRICULTURE IN THE YUNGAS

Between the Altiplano and the lowlands, fertile valleys known as the Yungas cut through the Andes. The high Yungas have a subtropical climate, and here farmers can produce bananas, pineapples, avocados, and other fruits. The timber includes mahogany, walnut, and chona (the source of quinine). The lower Yungas are used to grow sugarcane, coffee, cocoa, and tobacco. It is also here that coca leaves—the source of cocaine— have become an important but illegal crop, supplying a large part of the world's cocaine and massively boosting the country's ailing economy.

PARAGUAY

A small landlocked state in the center of South America, Paraguay is divided into two very distinct halves by the Paraguay River which flows north–south through the country. By far the largest part of the population lives in the eastern part. Paraguay's recent history has been scarred by two reckless and bloody wars with its neighbors, coupled with a long rule by a government that has a poor human rights record.

Geography

The western region of Paraguay is known as the Región Occidental. It forms part of the Gran Chaco, which extends into Bolivia and Argentina. The area is a vast, river-drained alluvial land with swamps, grassland, and scrub forests. Near the Paraguay River

NATIONAL DATA – PARAGUAY

Land area	397,300 sq km (153,398 sq mi)			
Climate	Altitude m (ft)	Temperatures January °C(°F)	July °C(°F)	Annual precipitation mm (in)
Asunción	139 (456)	23 (73)	18 (64)	1,404 (55.2)

Major physical features	highest point: Mount San Rafael 850 m (2,789 ft)

Population (2006 est.) 6,506,464

Form of government multiparty republic with two legislative houses

Armed forces army 7,600; navy 1,600; air force 1,100

Largest cities Asunción (capital - 506,094); Ciudad del Este (287,311); San Lorenzo* (245,468); Luque* (239,842); Capiatá* (232,831); Lambaré* (130,168); Fernando de la Mora* (123,620)   (* adjacent to Asunción)

Official languages Spanish, Guarani

Ethnic composition Mestizo (mixed Spanish and Amerindian) 95%; other 5%

Religious affiliations Roman Catholic 90%; Mennonite and other Protestant 10%

Currency 1 guarani (PYG) = 100 centimos

Gross domestic product (2006) $30.64 billion

Gross domestic product per capita (2006) U.S. $4,700

Life expectancy at birth male 72.56 yr; female 77.78 yr

Major resources hydropower, timber, iron ore, manganese, limestone, cassava, cattle, coffee, cotton, fruit, maize/corn, rice, soybeans, sugarcane, tobacco

the terrain consists of open forest and marshland. Huge cattle ranches dominate this region. In the extreme northwest, near the border with Bolivia, the land is covered with a thick forest of thorn trees. Only a small percentage of the population lives on the Chaco. The eastern region—the Región Oriental—rises gently from the floodplains of the Paraguay and Paraná Rivers to a series of low mountain chains that form part of the Brazilian plateau. In the region east of the Paraguay River there are rolling hills, grasslands, and woodland. The capital, Asunción, lies on the Paraguay River, near to the border with Argentina.

The climate of Paraguay is subtropical with seasonal rainfall. It is heaviest in the east, which is prone to flooding, but sparse in the west, where droughts are frequent. The country has large forests—although they are disappearing fast—and hardwood species grow in the eastern hills. Paraguay's wildlife includes peccaries, jaguars, anteaters, armadillos, and many species of birds, insects, and snakes.

History

The first European settlers to Paraguay lived peaceably with the indigenous Guaraní peoples, although later slave traders did not treat them so well. In 1776 Paraguay became part of the Viceroyalty of Río de la Plata, centered on Buenos Aires, but resentment at this eventually led to independence in 1811, followed by the establishment of a dictatorship under José Gaspar Rodríguez de Francia (1766–1840). Other dictatorships followed. Involvement in the War of the Triple Alliance (1865–70) ended in the country's

The Pantheon des los Heroes, Asuncion. Modeled on Les Invalides in Paris, construction started in 1863. It was halted the following year by the Chaco War and wasn't completed until 1936. It contains the tombs of Lopez and the Unkown Soldier from the Chaco War.

THE PEOPLE OF PARAGUAY

The population of Paraguay is found mainly in the eastern region; most people live within 160 km (100 mi) of the capital, Asunción. The Chaco region supports only about 2 percent of the people. Paraguay has one of the most homogeneous populations in South America. Over 90 percent of people are of mixed Spanish and Guaraní descent. There is little trace now of the original Guaraní culture, except in the language, which is understood by most of the population. Among other nationalities that have settled in Paraguay are Brazilians, Argentines, Germans, Arabs, Koreans, Chinese, and Japanese.

devastation, loss of territory, the deaths of many citizens, and occupation by the Brazilian army. Paraguay fought the equally disastrous Chaco War (1932–35) with Bolivia over Chaco land believed to contain oil. Many more lives were lost, and although land was gained, the oil never materialized. The 35-year reign of hardline military dictator General Alfredo Stroessner (1912–2006) ended when he was overthrown in 1989, heralding democratic elections.

Economy

Paraguay has a market economy with a service-based formal sector as well as a large informal sector involved with the reexport of consumer goods to neighboring countries. Agriculture employs one-quarter of the workforce, and although cattle ranching is the chief activity, crops such as soybeans and timber are also important. There are no significant mineral resources in Paraguay—almost uniquely in South America. Power comes in the form of cheap hydroelectricity from installations on the Paraná River, notably the Yacyreta-Agipe Dam (the world's largest). The hydroelectricity, which has stimulated industry, supplies domestic needs and also provides for exports. Commercial privatization has increased since 2000, but there is great inequality in wealth, and 36 percent of the population lives below the poverty line. Water and road transportation are well developed in the country. Healthcare and sanitation are adequate in the capital but poor elsewhere.

URUGUAY

Uruguay, South America's second smallest country, lies on the east coast of the continent. Known locally as the Banda Oriental, or "East Bank" (of the Uruguay River), the country was also more poetically dubbed "the Switzerland of South America" after the country's reputation for neutrality, prosperity, and harmony. For many years during the 20th century it had a democratic government and a high standard of living. However, it later briefly suffered all the ills of other troubled South American states—urban guerrilla attacks, military rule, a failing economy, and massive inflation.

NATIONAL DATA – URUGUAY

Land area   173,620 sq km (67,035 sq mi)

Climate	Altitude m (ft)	Temperatures January °C(°F)	July °C(°F)	Annual precipitation mm (in)
Montevideo	22 (72)	23 (73)	11 (52)	1101 (43.3)

Major physical features   highest point: Mount Catedral 514 m (1,685 ft)

Population   (2006 est.) 3,431,932

Form of government   multiparty republic with two legislative houses

Armed forces   army 15,200; navy 5,700; air force 3,100

Largest cities   Montevideo (capital - 1,272,411); Salto (101,318); Paysandú (73,135); Las Piedras (70,571); Rivera (65,010); Maldonado (57,205); Tacuarembó (53,147); Melo (51,925)

Official language   Spanish

Ethnic composition   White 88%; Mestizo 8%; Black 4%

Religious affiliations   Roman Catholic 66%; Protestant 2%; Jewish 1%; nonprofessing or other 31%

Currency   1 Uruguayan peso (UYU) = 100 centesimos

Gross domestic product   (2006) U.S. $36.56 billion

Gross domestic product per capita   (2006) U.S. $10,700

Life expectancy at birth   male 73.12 yr; female 79.65 yr

Major resources   hydropower, fisheries, amethysts, barley, cattle, maize/corn, marble, rice, sheep, topaz, wheat

Geography

Uruguay is sandwiched in a transitional region between the uplands of Brazil to the north and the humid Argentinian pampas to the west. The landscape of Uruguay is predominantly low-lying, apart from two ranges of hills, including the Cuchilla Grande, that extend southward from the Brazilian border. Most of Uruguay is covered in lush grassland. Trees are few in number, and grow mainly along the banks of rivers. The natural vegetation is tall pampas grass, with only a few shrubs and flowers. The country's climate is mild and temperate, and there is plentiful rainfall throughout the year. The Rio de la Plata estuary forms a huge border in the south, while the Uruguay River extends the length of the border with Argentina. The other major waterway is the Negro River, which runs east to west across the whole country.

Uruguay's wildlife is varied but no longer abundant—extensive cattle grazing on the grasslands

Much of Uruguay's landscape consists of rich, rolling pampas grasslands dotted with trees.

having altered the habitat to the detriment of much of the native fauna and flora. Mammalian life includes armadillos and capybaras. Birds are relatively abundant and include the burrowing owls of the pampas as well as many aquatic species.

History

In 1726 the Spanish founded Montevideo, driving out earlier Portuguese settlers as well as exterminating the original Charrúa Amerindians. In 1776 the country was incorporated into the Viceroyalty of Río de la Plata. Brazilian-Portuguese occupation followed, but this was ended in 1828 with Argentinian and British help, and Uruguay became independent. Civil war and unrest ensued for many years, with either civilian or military governments ruling. A period of prosperity and unity

was followed by economic collapse in the 1930s, and a dictatorship. Uruguay was neutral during World War II, which heralded an economic boom. More economic problems then fueled a campaign in the 1960s by violent urban Marxist guerrillas known as the Tupumaros, leading to a military takeover of the country in the 1970s. Gradual civilian rule was restored in 1985. Conditions for Uruguay's political and labor movements are at present among the freest in South America.

Economy

Much of Uruguay's land is suitable for agriculture, but only a small percentage is cultivated; most of the vast rolling grassland is used instead to graze livestock such as herds of cattle and flocks of sheep. Crops include rice, wheat, maize/corn, and barley. Once the mainstay of the economy, agriculture's share of export earnings has fallen back as new industries such as tourism and electricity generation have expanded.

Uruguay has no natural mineral resources, and manufacturing—which is also expanding—is based on imported raw materials. There is a growing iron and steel industry. Paper, aluminum, cement, polyethylene, transportation equipment, textiles, beverages and chemicals are also produced. Uruguay's main trading partners are Brazil, Argentina, Mexico, Spain, and Germany. The vigorous economy benefits from having a well-educated workforce, and the country also has good welfare and healthcare systems.

EUROPEAN-STYLE MONTEVIDEO

Montevideo, the capital of Uruguay, is situated on the northern bank of the River Plate. It was founded in 1726 by Spanish settlers, and expanded to become the center of the meat industry and later the financial center and main trading port. Successive waves of Italian and Spanish immigrants have made the city's population almost completely European. Montevideo also has a European architectural heritage with stately 19th-century buildings and shady squares. The parks and gardens, coupled with the Mediterranean climate, add to the European atmosphere.

ARGENTINA

The name Argentina comes from the Latin meaning "land of silver," and the country has long attracted settlers in search of wealth. Its natural resources and human endeavors have helped make Argentina a modern country, but social and economic development have been held back by a history of political instability.

NATIONAL DATA – ARGENTINA

Land area	2,736,690 sq km (1,056,642 sq mi)			
Climate	Altitude m (ft)	Temperatures January °C(°F)	July °C(°F)	Annual precipitation mm (in)
Buenos Aires	25 (82)	25 (74)	12 (90)	1,205 (47.4)

Major physical features highest point: Aconcagua 6,960 m (22,834 ft); longest river: Paraná (part) 4,500 km (2,800 mi)

Population (2006 est.) 39,921,833

Form of government federal multiparty republic with two legislative houses

Armed forces army 41,400; navy 17,500; air force 12,500

Largest cities Buenos Aires (capital – 11,612,214); Córdoba (1,475,447); Rosario (1,178,407); Mendoza (890,521)

Official language Spanish

Ethnic composition White (mostly Spanish and Italian) 97%; Mestizo (mixed White and Amerindian ancestry); Amerindian, or other non-white groups 3%

Religious affiliations Roman Catholic 92% (less than 20% practicing); Protestant 2%; Jewish 2%; other 4%

Currency 1 Argentine peso (ARS) = 100 centavos

Gross domestic product (2006) U.S. $599.1 billion

Gross domestic product per capita (2006) U.S. $15,000

Life expectancy at birth male 72.38 yr; female 80.05 yr

Major resources aluminum, cement, lead, zinc, tin, copper, hydropower, iron ore, manganese, petroleum, uranium, apples, cattle, citrus fruits, coal, cotton, fruit, fish, grapes, gold, limestone, maize/corn, mica, natural gas, olives, potatoes, peanuts, rice, sheep, silver, sorghum, soybeans, sugarcane, sunflower seeds, timber, tungsten, tobacco, wheat, wool

Geography

Argentina's scenery differs greatly from north to south, and there is also a marked contrast between the lofty mountains of the west and the broad plains in the east. The impenetrable Andes Mountains run the length of the western border with Chile, and beyond. Some are volcanic, including Aconcagua, South America's highest peak. Earthquakes are common. In the north, bordering Paraguay, are the poorly drained, subtropical scrublands of the Gran Chaco. Southeast of here, between the Paraná and Uruguay Rivers, is the low-lying rain-forest region of Mesopotamia. South of Mesopotamia the flat fertile plains of the pampas extend southeast to meet the Atlantic coast south of the River Plate. This area is the most highly populated part of Argentina. The southernmost part of Argentina is Patagonia—a barren and arid plateau, but rich in minerals.

Most of the country lies within the southern temperate zone, although the northeastern plains are subtropical, and the extreme south is subpolar. Rainfall is light and falls mainly in Mesopotamia, the Chaco, and the pampas. Wildlife includes llamas, monkeys, jaguars, armadillos, and snakes. Birds range from toucans and parrots to hummingbirds and ostrichlike rheas. In the rivers there are many fish, including voracious piranhas. Sea lions are found off the coast.

Society

From the 16th century to the present Argentinian society has been shaped by the culture of its European colonists. Until the mid-20th century much of Argentina's history was punctuated by periods of internal political conflict between civilian and military factions and between conservatives and liberals. Following World War II, Domingo Perón (1895–1974) emerged as a popular leader, establishing social reforms and economic stability, before he was deposed in 1955. He was recalled from exile in 1973 but died a year later. His wife Isabel (b. 1931) took over but was overthrown

THE LIFE OF THE GAUCHOS

The Argentinian pampas is one of the traditional homes of the gaucho—more or less the equivalent of the cowboy of the American West. Tough, resourceful, and excellent horsemen, the gauchos are mostly mestizos who have little regard for the refined ways of city dwellers. Employed on the huge ranches that sprawl across the vast open plains of the pampas, the gaucho's task is to herd cattle. Gauchos traditionally wear distinctive loose-fitting trousers (known as *bombachas*), a scarf wrapped around the waist and between the legs (a *chiripá*), and a flat-topped hat.

in a coup in 1976, and there followed seven years of oppressive military rule. In 1982 the defeat of Argentina by Britain in the war over sovereignty of the Falklands caused a return to democratic government in 1983, which has persisted despite challenges.

Economy

Although Argentina has a free-market economy and is rich in resources, high inflation and foreign debt have led to severe economic problems, and there has been large-scale emigration to Spain. More than half the total land area is farmland, and much of this is pasture. Beef production, the traditional mainstay, is centered on the huge ranches of the pampas. Sheep, pigs, and goats are also raised, and wool is exported. The chief crops are wheat, maize/corn, soybeans, and sugarcane. Vegetable oils, animal feedstuffs, fish, and fish oil make up other exports. Argentina is almost self-sufficient in power, the main sources being hydroelectricity, natural gas, and petroleum. There also several nuclear power plants. About one-fifth of the workforce is involved in manufacturing, of which food processing is a major sector. There is a growing iron and steel industry, and paper, aluminum, cement, and polyethylene are produced in significant quantities.

Argentina has the best transportation system in South America, with well-developed roads, railroads, shipping, and air travel. Social welfare problems exist, in particular in housing. This is often stretched to capacity in cities, to which workers migrate in search of work. Health standards vary across the country.

The broad open landscape of fertile grasslands rising to hills around Balcarce, situated about 290 km (180 mi) south of Buenos Aires.

CHILE

Chile measures on average little more than 160 km (100 mi) from east to west, but extends south from the tropics to within about 966 km (600 mi) of Antarctica. Chile was one of the first South American countries to adopt democratic political and economic structures, but suffered from military rule in recent times.

Geography

The land divides lengthways into the coastal mountains, the Andes ranges, and the long trench between them. The whole country is subject to earthquakes. The coastal ranges run from near the Peruvian border south to central-southern Chile. Onward from here they are partly submerged, their peaks forming islands. The central trench extends from the Atacama Desert salt flats in the north to the Gulf of Ancud. The central-southern section is known as the Central Valley; this is the most populous part of Chile and is the site of the capital, Santiago. The highest peaks of the huge Andean cordillera are in the north and center, where active volcanoes are also found. The southern Andes have a glaciated landscape of lakes and fjords, and the extreme south forms numerous islands, including Tierra del Fuego and Cape Horn, the southernmost point.

NATIONAL DATA – CHILE

Land area	748,800 sq km (289,113 sq mi)			

Climate	Altitude m (ft)	Temperatures January °C(°F)	July °C(°F)	Annual precipitation mm (in)
Santiago	520 (1,706)	22 (72)	9 (48)	313 (12.3)

Major physical features	highest point: Llullaillaco 6,723 m (22,057 ft)

Population	(2006 est.) 16,134,219

Form of government	multiparty republic with two legislative houses

Armed forces	army 47,700; navy 19,398; air force 11,000

Largest cities	Santiago (capital – 4,949,540); Valparaíso (287,194); Concepción (666,381); La Serena (159,081); Antofagasta (319,422)

Official language	Spanish

Ethnic composition	White and White-Amerindian 95%; Amerindian 3%; other 2%

Religious affiliations	Roman Catholic 89%; Protestant 11%; some Jewish

Currency	1 Chilean peso (CLP) = 100 centavos

Gross domestic product	(2006) U.S. $203 billion

Gross domestic product per capita	(2006) U.S. $12,600

Life expectancy at birth	male 73.49 yr; female 80.21 yr

Major resources	copper, timber, iron ore, nitrates, precious metals, molybdenum, hydropower, natural gas, petroleum, beans, coal, fish, fruit, grapes, lead, livestock, maize/corn, manganese, oil, onions, potatoes, rice, sugar beet, wheat, wine, zinc

The climate is mainly temperate but ranges from tropical to antarctic. There is almost no rain in the Atacama Desert. The south experiences strong winds and high rainfall. Plant life is varied, according to climate and topography, and includes monkey puzzle and tamarugo trees. Animals include pumas, vicuñas, and guanacos. The magnificent but endangered Andean condor lives high in the mountains.

Society

Before Spanish settlers arrived in the 16th century, Chile was inhabited by Incas and Araucanian peoples; the latter were not fully subjugated until the 1880s. Chile declared independence in 1818 after bitter struggles against the Spanish. In the War of the Pacific (1879–84) Chile gained large areas of land from Peru and Bolivia, securing the rich nitrate deposits of the Atacama Desert. The three-year-old Marxist government of Salvador Allende Gossens (1908–73) was overthrown in 1973 in a military coup led by General Augusto

The harsh mountainous landscape of northern Chile supports only sparse vegetation, which is grazed by hardy animals such as herds of llamas.

THE ATACAMA DESERT

Chile's Atacama Desert is an arid wasteland covering an area of 132,000 sq km (51,000 sq mi) in the north of the country, extending from the Pacific to the Andes. It has an average width of only 140 km (100 mi), but it extends 966 km (600 mi) south from the border with Peru. In some parts of the desert there was no rain from 1570 to 1971! The desert is made up of salt basins, sand, and lava. Despite its desolate nature, some hardy plants have adapted to this dry environment, and flocks of flamingoes feed on algae in the salt lakes. There is even a town, called Calama, in this inhospitable desert.

Pinochet Ugarte (1915–2006). He ruled until a freely elected president was installed in 1990. Chile has since assumed increasing regional and international leadership roles befitting its status as a democratic, stable country.

Economy

Chile is blessed with plentiful natural resources, although fluctuating market prices have made it economically vulnerable, and it has thus increasingly developed its manufacturing base. Sound economic policies since the 1980s have enabled Chile to maintain steady growth, unlike most other Latin American countries. Agriculture flourishes, although much food is imported. Arable farming is centered on the fertile Central Valley, and crops include wheat, potatoes, and rice. Fruit, vegetables, and wine are exported. The main livestock animals are sheep and beef cattle. Fish stocks off the coast are plentiful; sardines and anchovies are among the main catches. Forestry is a source of timber and paper products. Chile leads the world in copper exports. Other minerals include iron and molybdenum. The main energy source is hydroelectric power, supplemented by coal, petroleum, and natural gas. Manufacturing includes iron, steel, and petroleum refining, fish processing, and petrochemicals.

The country has a well-established health service. The welfare system is equally well developed. Education is free up to the age of 17, and literacy levels are high.

FALKLAND ISLANDS

Overseas Territory of United Kingdom

The Falkland Islands are a self-governing colony in the South Atlantic Ocean comprising an archipelago off the southeastern coast of South America. The Falkland Islands themselves administer a collection of island dependencies which include the volcanic South Sandwich Islands as well as South Georgia—a former whaling settlement and the largest of the dependencies. The islands of East and West Falkland make up most of the land area. Heavily indented, hilly, and often swept by cold westerly winds, both islands are mostly covered in peaty moorland, with low grasses, scrubby vegetation, and no trees. Animal life includes elephant seals, sea lions, and penguins.

The islands were first sighted by British navigators in 1592. The British established a garrison here in 1765 but disbanded it in 1774, although they maintained their claim to the islands. In 1820 the newly independent Argentina claimed the islands—which it called the Islas Malvinas—marking the start of a long-running dispute over sovereignty between Britain and Argentina. In 1833, after a failed attempt by Argentina to settle the islands, the British reestablished a garrison. An almost completely British population then became established, with a limited economy based—as it is today—on fishing and sheep rearing.

In 1892 colonial government was introduced, with a governor appointed by the British monarch. Argentina continued to press its claims, however, and in 1982 it invaded the Falklands. In response, Britain launched a large task force to retake the islands. After six weeks of fierce fighting, the British expelled the occupying forces. Hostilities were formally ended in 1989, but Argentina still lays claim to the islands—in part, it is suggested, as a way of deflecting attention away from its own poor record of government at home. The local economy has been affected by the Falklands War and its aftermath. An exclusion zone was created around the islands to prevent overfishing (fishing licences are now the island's biggest source of income), and an enlarged military presence and an influx of tourists (attracted mainly by the wildlife) have boosted the economy. A 320-km (200-mi) oil exploration zone was imposed in 1993.

FRENCH GUIANA

Overseas Department of France

French Guiana is a French overseas department lying just north of the equator on South America's northeast coast. To the west it is bordered by Suriname, and to the east and south by Brazil. There are two main geographical areas: the lowlying coastal plains, and the forested plateau of the interior that rises to form mountains along the southern border. The climate is hot and humid with frequent rain. Most people live on the coast, which is fertile but swampy. There is savanna in the west, but most of the country is covered by impenetrable hardwood forests that support a wide variety of wildlife. Cayenne, now the capital, was founded by French merchants in 1643, but other

European colonists frustrated their attempts at colonization. By the late 17th century, however, the French had established a colony, and imported slaves to work the plantations. After the French Revolution (1789–99) political prisoners were sent here to die in appalling conditions.

Following the abolition of slavery in the 1850s the economy collapsed. French missionaries set up educational institutions for freed slaves. Penal settlements were again established, including the notorious Devil's Island, immortalized by the harrowing experiences recounted by Henri Charrière (1906–73) in

Huge statues carved from soft volcanic rock stare out across the sea at Playa de Anakena on remote Easter Island.

his novel *Papillon*. The bleak penal settlements were not disbanded until after World War II.

French Guianans have enjoyed French citizenship since 1848 and parliamentary representation since 1870. However, moves toward independence have not met with any great success. The population numbers about 200,000. Most people are of mixed descent, speaking French and Creole, and the main religion is Roman Catholicism. The Maroons, descendants of escaped African slaves, live mainly along the Maroni River. Up to 4 percent of the population is Amerindian, for example, the Arawak. The Maroons and some Amerindian groups still practice their own religion. French Guiana is economically dependent on France. Agriculture, concentrated in the coastal region, produces staples and cash crops such as bananas and sugarcane. Fish are also exported, as are gold and bauxite. The European Space Agency has a launch site at Kourou.

EASTER ISLAND
Territory of Chile

The tiny, remote volcanic Easter Island, some 3,780 km (2,350 mi) west of the South American coast, was annexed to Chile in 1888. The island was named by the Dutch admiral Jacob Roggeveen (1659–1729), who landed there on Easter Sunday 1722. Before Europeans discovered it, the island had a thriving Polynesian community which left behind some spectacular ancient monuments. Most are monolithic statues and huge faces carved from stone, some standing up to 20 m (65 ft) tall and weighing 50 tons. The oldest may have been there for 1,000 years, but the most recent originate from the 17th century. Few of the stone carvers' descendants survive on the island today; Peruvian slave raids in 1862–63, coupled with major epidemics, almost wiped out the Polynesian population. Christian missionaries in the 19th century contributed further to the decline of the indigenous culture. The island was then repopulated with Spanish speakers from the mainland. Most of the 1,400 inhabitants today live in the village of Hanga Roa on the sheltered western coast. They earn a traditional living by sheep ranching, which generates trade in wool, but since the mid-1980s the main income has been derived from tourism.

INDONESIA

The republic of Indonesia forms a long island bridge between the Asian continent and Australia. It consists of an archipelago of 13,677 islands extending 5,100 km (3,200 mi) from Sumatra to Papua (formerly Irian Jaya) on New Guinea. Parts of Borneo and New Guinea are shared with other countries.

Geography

Indonesia's islands are strewn over 8 million sq km (3 million sq mi) of tropical seas. The western section

forms part of the Sunda shelf—a mostly submerged extension of the Asian continent. The central section is part of a partially submerged mountain chain extending to the Philippines. The Sahul shelf in the east forms the northern extension of Australia. Borneo has forested highlands descending to flat swamplands. The island of Sumatra has forested lowlands rising to mountains and 10 active volcanoes. Java is mountainous and heavily populated. Sulawesi Island has mountainous peninsulas radiating from a highland core. Northern New Guinea is mountainous, but the south has low-lying swampland. The whole archipelago lies on or near the equator and has high temperatures all year, but the highlands are cooler. Inland, much of the archipelago is covered in forests that are among the world's richest habitats but in places they have been devastated by logging and settlement. The Komodo dragon, the world's largest lizard, is one of the region's unique animals.

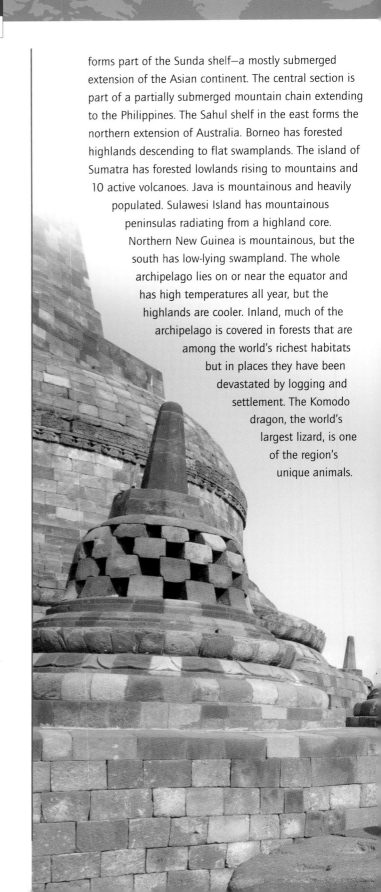

NATIONAL DATA – INDONESIA

Land area	1,826,440 sq km (705,192 sq mi)			

Climate		Temperatures		Annual
	Altitude m (ft)	January °C(°F)	July °C(°F)	precipitation mm (in)
Jakarta	8 (26)	27 (81)	29 (84)	1,659 (65.3)

Major physical features highest point: Mount Jaya (New Guinea) 5,040 m (16,535 ft); longest river: Barito (Borneo) 885 km (550 mi); largest lake: Lake Toba (Sumatra) 1,300 sq km (502 sq mi)

Population (2006 est.) 245,452,739

Form of government multiparty republic with two legislative houses

Armed forces army 233,000; navy 45,000; air force 24,000

Largest cities Jakarta (capital - 8,568,838); Surabaya (2,358,111); Bandung (1,651,840); Medan (1,763,874); Bekasi (1,619,775); Palembang (1,257,449)

Official language Bahasa Indonesian

Ethnic composition Javanese 45%; Sundanese 14%; Madurese 7.5%; Coastal Malays 7.5%; other 26%

Religious affiliations Muslim 88%; Protestant 5%; Roman Catholic 3%; Hindu 2%; Buddhist 1%; other 1%

Currency 1 Indonesian rupiah (IDR) = 100 sen

Gross domestic product (2006) U.S. $935 billion

Gross domestic product per capita (2006) U.S. $3,800

Life expectancy at birth male 67.42 yr; female 72.45 yr

Major resources petroleum, tin, natural gas, nickel, timber, bauxite, copper, coal, gold, silver, bananas, cassava, copra, coffee, fish, ground nut, maize/corn, palm oil, rice, rubber, soybeans, spices, sugarcane, sweet potatoes, tea, tobacco

INDONESIA'S DIVERSE PEOPLES

The Indonesians comprise 200 to 300 ethnic groups, most of which probably have Austronesian (Malayo-Polynesian) ancestry. The exceptions are the Papuan peoples of New Guinea, who are Australoid in origin, like the Aboriginals. The Javanese are the dominant ethnic group, although the official language—Bahasa Indonesia—is based on an east Sumatran form of Malay that spread to Malaya and coastal Borneo; most educated people speak it as a second language. The only significant immigrant population are the ethnic Chinese. Most people are Muslims.

Society

The Indonesian archipelago is one of the oldest inhabited areas on Earth; human beings lived there over 500,000 years ago. The ancestors of most Indonesians probably arrived from Asia in about 1000 B.C. The Portuguese and then the Dutch colonized the area in the 16th century. Indonesia declared its independence after World War II. Home to the world's largest Muslim population, Indonesia suffered a devastating tsunami in 2004, followed later by earthquakes. It also faces difficulties over human rights, defeating terrorism, and a separatist movement in Papua. Further unrest has been caused by the resettlement of many Javanese to outlying islands, where they often outnumber the original inhabitants.

Economy

The economy suffered greatly in the 1997 Asian financial crisis but it later improved, only to be hit by the effects of the 2004 tsunami. Agriculture employs about 40 percent of the workforce, producing about 20 percent of GDP. Rice is the major crop, but staples such as cassava and soybeans are also grown. Cash crops include rubber, tea, coffee, and spices. The vast forests have supplied much timber in the past, but there is international concern over the exploitation of this resource. Sumatra, Borneo, and the Java Sea provide petroleum and natural gas for export and for fuel. The chief manufacturing sectors are chemicals, electronic components, rubber tires, and textiles. Shipping is the most effective means of transportation. Only Java has an adequate system of roads, but both Java and Sumatra have state-operated railroads.

The Borobudur temple complex, thought to date from around the beginning of the 8th century A.D., was the spiritual center of Buddhism in Java.

PAPUA NEW GUINEA

Papua New Guinea comprises the eastern portion of the island of New Guinea as well as numerous small islands to the north and east. Papua New Guinea is dominated by mountains that are subject to volcanic activity and earthquakes. The only extensive lowlands are on New Guinea island, around the huge Central Range. The climate is hot and humid, with heavy seasonal rainfall. Vegetation varies from coastal mangroves and lowland swamp forests to forests of oak, beech, and pine in upland areas. The wildlife includes many spectacular species, such as flightless cassowaries and the colorful birds of paradise. The people of Papua New Guinea are divided into two main groups—Papuan and Melanesian—but other groups are also found.

Papua New Guinea is rich in minerals, including gold and copper. The chief economic activity is mining, with minerals accounting for most of the exports. Natural gas, oil, and hydroelectricity supply power. Agriculture is mainly in the form of either subsistence farming or intensive production of commodities such as tea and coffee. Important forestry and fisheries exports include logs, lumber, palm oil, prawns, and tuna.

Dancers in ornate and colorful costumes performing at the Sing Sing festival at Mount Hagen in the heart of Papua New Guinea.

NATIONAL DATA – PAPUA NEW GUINEA

Land area   452,860 sq km (174,850 sq mi)

Climate	Altitude m (ft)	Temperatures January °C(°F)	July °C(°F)	Annual precipitation mm (in)
Port Moresby	38 (125)	28 (82)	26 (79)	1,112 (43.7)

Major physical features   highest point: Mount Wilhelm 4,508 m (14,790 ft); longest river: Sepik about 1,000 km (600 mi)

Population   (2006 est.) 5,670,544

Form of government   multiparty constitutional monarchy with one legislative house

Armed forces   army 2,500; air force 200

Capital city   Port Moresby (295,892)

Official language   English

Ethnic composition   Papuan 84%; Melanesian 15%; others 1%

Religious affiliations   Roman Catholic 22%; Lutheran 16%; Presbyterian/Methodist/London Missionary Society 8%; Anglican 5%; Evangelical Alliance 4%; Seventh-Day Adventist 1%; other Protestant 10%; traditional beliefs 34%

Currency   1 kina (PGK) = 100 toea

Gross domestic product   (2006) U.S. $15.13 billion

Gross domestic product per capita   (2006) U.S. $2,700

Life expectancy at birth   male 63.08 yr; female 67.58 yr

Major resources   gold, copper, silver, natural gas, timber, oil, hydropower, fisheries, bananas, cassava, cocoa, coconuts, coffee, rubber, sago, sugarcane, sweet potatoes, tea, vegetables, yams

EAST TIMOR

East Timor lies in southeastern Asia in the Lesser Sunda Islands at the eastern end of the Indonesian archipelago, and northwest of Australia. East Timor includes the eastern half of the island of Timor, the Oecussi (Ambeno) region on the northwest part of the island of Timor, and the tiny southern Pacific islands of Pulau Atauro and Pulau Jaco.

East Timor became an independent republic on May 20, 2002, after two years of UN Transitional Administration. The Portuguese colony of Timor declared independence from Portugal in 1975, but was invaded by Indonesian forces nine days later. In 1976 it was incorporated into Indonesia as East Timor, and there followed 25 years of brutal repression by Indonesian forces, resulting in the loss of one-quarter of the province's population through violence and famine.

In 1999 the new Indonesian government allowed East Timor to hold a referendum. Despite violence and intimidation at the polls, nearly 80 percent of the voters (about 450,000 people) chose independence. During 1999 to 2001 pro-Jakarta anti-independence militias began a violent campaign of arson and theft. By the time UN forces intervened, much of East Timor's infrastructure had been destroyed. In addition, some 260,000 people had fled westward. Over the next three years an international program began a massive reconstruction in both rural and urban areas.

The country is faced with enormous challenges, including continuing to rebuild the infrastructure and creating jobs. Agricultural products include coffee, rice, cassava, vanilla, and mangos. Coffee, sandalwood, and marble are exported. Industry is mainly based around the manufacture of soap, handicrafts, and woven cloth. A promising long-term project is the development of the offshore oil and gas fields in nearby waters, which it is hoped will generate much-needed revenues.

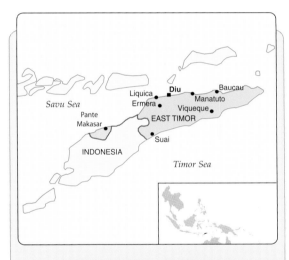

NATIONAL DATA – EAST TIMOR

Land area	15,007 sq km (5,794 sq mi)
Climate	tropical with monsoon rain and pronounced dry season
Major physical features	highest point: Mount Tata Mailau or Ramelau 2,950 m (9,679 ft)
Population	(2006 est.) 1,062,777
Form of government	multiparty republic with one legislative house
Armed forces	army 1,250; naval element 36
Capital city	Dili (166,903)
Official languages	Tetum, Portuguese
Ethnic composition	Timorese 78% (including Maubere); Indonesian 20%; Chinese 2%
Religious affiliations	Roman Catholic 90%; Muslim 4%; Protestant 3%; Hindu 0.5%; Buddhist; Animist 2.5%
Currency	1 lira (Lit) = 100 centesimi
Life expectancy at birth	male 63.96 yr; female 68.67 yr
Major resources	fish, timber, maize/corn, rice, cassava, sweet potatoes, coffee, coconuts, vanilla, mangoes, livestock, gold, petroleum, natural gas, manganese, marble

AUSTRALIA

The smallest continent, but still a huge landmass, Australia is about one-third desert. As well as being the

NATIONAL DATA – AUSTRALIA

Land area   7,617,930 sq km (2,941,299 sq mi)

Climate	Altitude m (ft)	Temperatures January °C(°F)	July °C(°F)	Annual precipitation mm (in)
Darwin	27 (89)	28 (81)	25 (77)	1,708 (67.2)
Alice Springs	548 (1,797)	29 (84)	12 (54)	289 (11.3)
Sydney	42 (138)	22 (72)	12 (54)	1,222 (48.1)

Major physical features   highest point: Monte Kosciusko 2,228 m (7,310 ft); lowest point: Lake Eyre –16m (–52 ft); longest river: Murray-Darling 3,717 km (2,310 mi)

Population   (2006 est.) 20,264,082

Form of government   federal multiparty parliamentary state with two legislative houses

Armed forces   army 26,035; navy 14,070; air force 15,670

Largest cities   Sydney (4,490,662); Melbourne (3,829,400); Brisbane (1,938,851); Perth (1,497,487); Adelaide (1,079,558); Gold Coast (546,025); Canberra (capital – 325,888); Newcastle (502,338); Wollongong (262,894)

Official language   English

Ethnic composition   Caucasian 92%; Asian 7%; Aboriginal and other 1%

Religious affiliations   Catholic 26.4%; Anglican 20.5%; other Christian 20.5%; Buddhist 1.9%; Muslim 1.5%; other 1.2%; unspecified 12.7%; none 15.3%

Currency   1 Australian dollar (AUD) = 100 cents

Gross domestic product   (2006) U.S. $666.3 billion

Gross domestic product per capita   (2006) U.S. $32,900

Life expectancy at birth   male 77.64 yr; female 83.52 yr

Major resources   bauxite, coal, iron ore, copper, tin, gold, silver, uranium, nickel, tungsten, mineral sands, lead, zinc, natural gas, petroleum, barley, cattle, diamonds, fish, fruit, maize/corn, manganese, oats, opals, pigs, rice, rutile, sheep, sorghum, sugarcane, timber, tobacco, tourism, vegetables, wheat, wine, wool

driest continent, it is also the least mountainous. It was the last continent to be discovered and settled by Europeans; the indigenous peoples were the Aboriginals, who were hunter-gatherers.

Geography
Australia can be divided into three regions. The Great Plateau, which occupies more than half the country, rises near the west coast and drops gently eastward into the arid "red center," named for the red-brown landscape. Between the plateau edge and the Musgrave Range lies Uluru, the world's biggest single rock. The central eastern lowlands consist of three artesian basins separated by upland ridges. East of the central lowlands the land rises to the Great Dividing Range, then drops steeply toward the coastal plains, where over half the population lives. From northern Queensland to the south coast of Victoria the highlands run parallel to the shoreline. The climate ranges from tropical to temperate over this vast landscape.

Society
Before Europeans discovered Australia, the country was inhabited by Aboriginal peoples, who probably came from Southeast Asia about 50,000 years ago. Dutch seamen were in all likelihood the first Europeans to set eyes on Australia, in 1606. Captain James Cook (1728–79) discovered and named Botany Bay in 1770. Soon after, the British began to use the region as a penal colony, but the practice of transportation ceased in 1868. The discovery of gold in 1851 brought new settlers. After World War II many new European migrants arrived. In 1973 the country relaxed its "White Australia" immigration policy and, as a result, many Asian groups have also chosen to live in the country. Perhaps because of their geographical isolation, Australians tend to be confident, outgoing people with great belief in the values and virtues of their country.

Economy
Australia's early wealth was based on its extensive mineral resources and vast areas of farmland. Since World War II the country has focused on processing its minerals, but it also exports raw materials, especially

Two of Sydney's most famous waterside landmarks—the stunning Opera House, on the left, and the Harbour Bridge.

to Japan, which is highly industrialized but lacks resources. Australia's manufacturing sector—iron and steel, machinery, refining, electronics, and textiles—faces stiff competition from its Southeast Asian neighbors.

Much of the country's farmland is better suited to grazing than crops, and vast ranches, known as stations, rear over 26 million cattle per year, with most beef exported to the United States. Australia is the world's leading wool producer, and there are more than 120 million sheep in Australia, mostly grazed on the poorer scrubland. The varied climate enables a wide range of fruit and vegetables to be grown. Forestry, fishing, and wine production are also important. Tourism and service industries are expanding. Most domestic freight is carried by road, and there is heavy investment in road building. Railroads, ships, and aircraft are important methods of transportation for goods and people.

AUSTRALIA'S UNIQUE MAMMALS

Australia has two kinds of unusual mammals. Animals such as kangaroos, wallabies, koalas, possums, and bandicoots are marsupials. Instead of developing in a placenta within the mother's body like most mammals, young marsupials are born in a very undeveloped state and then continue their development in an external pouch known as a marsupium. Marsupials are also found in New Guinea, and the American opossum is found in North and South America. Unique to Australia and New Guinea are the platypus and the echidna. Both of these mammals produce young by laying eggs.

Australia is a federation of six states, two mainland territories, and additional island territories—only a few of which are inhabited.

Queensland

The most northeasterly Australian state, Queensland covers an area of 1,272,200 sq km (591,200 sq mi). Split into two by the Great Dividing Range, the fertile coastal plain has a hot, monsoon-type climate, whereas the interior is dry. Off the coast, the Great Barrier Reef—the world's largest coral structure—extends for 2,300 km (1,400 mi) and supports a rich and varied marine life. The state has tropical and subtropical forests along the coastal region, inhabited by animals such as koalas, tree frogs, skinks, and lorikeets. The state has large reserves of coal, bauxite, silver, copper, lead, and zinc. Farming products include pineapples, cereals, sugarcane, and cattle. The state capital is Brisbane.

New South Wales

The most populated state—with over 6,730,000 inhabitants—New South Wales covers an area of 801,430 sq km (309, 433 sq mi). The state is also Australia's most urbanized. The capital, Sydney, is Australia's largest city and is situated around the huge and attractive Sydney Harbour. A fertile coastal region lies to the east of the Great Dividing Range, but the far western plains are semiarid. The state has reserves of coal as well as zinc, lead, and silver. New South Wales has a growing wine industry. Other farming produce includes wheat, fruit, dairy products, cattle, and sheep.

Victoria

The state of Victoria, whose capital is Melbourne, covers an area of 227,600 sq km (88,875 sq mi) in the extreme southwest of Australia. Victoria was once part of New South Wales, but it became a separate colony in 1851. Inland from the Great Dividing Range there are arable and grazing plains where wheat, sheep, and cattle are the most important commodities. Victoria is an important industrial state; the gold reserves found at Bendigo and Ballarat fueled a gold rush in 1851, but now the chief resources are brown coal, and petroleum and natural gas which are found off the coast.

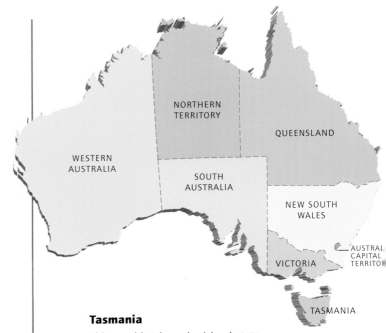

Tasmania

This roughly triangular island state covers an area of 68,330 sq km (26,380 sq mi). Tasmania, whose capital is Hobart, was named for Dutch explorer Abel Janszoon Tasman (c.1603–59), who discovered it in 1642. In 1803 the British took it over as a penal colony. Tasmania's terrain is mountainous, and it has a moist, temperate climate that encourages varied vegetation, including evergreen eucalyptus forest, temperate rain forest, and alpine heathland. Tasmania was the last stronghold of the unique marsupial wolf, or thylacine, until its extinction. Industries include forestry and paper manufacture, and many Tasmanians are employed in the service sectors. Agricultural products include potatoes and apples. Sheep and cattle are also reared. Seafood exports, such as abalone, salmon, and crayfish are important. The topography and climate of Tasmania enable much of its power to be generated by hydroelectricity.

South Australia

The state of South Australia is 984,380 sq km (380,070 sq mi) in area. More than 60 percent of the population lives in the state capital, Adelaide. The southeast has significant rain, but

inland and to the west, agricultural land gives way to scrub and then desert. Mineral reserves include natural gas and petroleum, located in the northeast. Iron ore, silver, and lead are also found. The state produces many kinds of fruit, and wine exports are on the increase.

Western Australia

Occupying the western third of the continent, Australia's largest state is 2,525,500 sq km (975,100 sq mi) in area. Founded in 1829, it was the second British colony in Australia. Most of the land is flat and very dry, although the Kimberley Plateau and the Pilbara, in the northwest, are upland regions. Situated on the Swan River, the state capital, Perth, contains three-quarters of the population. Western Australia has rich mineral resources, especially gold, iron, nickel, natural gas, and alumina. It is the world's third-largest iron ore producer. Agricultural exports include wheat, barley, and sheep products such as wool and meat. As in other parts of Australia, tourism has grown in importance; the majority of visitors come from Britain and the Far East.

Northern Territory

Situated in the north-central region of Australia, one-third of this territory is

Uluru (Ayers Rock) is a 600 million-year-old outcrop of rock southwest of Alice Springs in the Northern Territory. Sacred to the Aboriginal peoples, it is over 300 m (1,100 ft) high.

Aboriginal land. The capital is Darwin, and other sizeable towns include Alice Springs and Katherine. The climate is tropical, and most of the semiarid land is covered with scrub, which is used for livestock rearing and mining. Mineral resources include large deposits of manganese, bauxite, iron ore, and uranium. The Northern Territory has an area of 1,346,200 sq km (519,770 sq mi).

Australian Capital Territory

The region around the country's capital, Canberra, is known as the Australian Capital Territory. It covers an area of 2,432 sq km (939 sq mi) southwest of Sydney. The main farming activity is sheep rearing.

NEW ZEALAND

The island state of New Zealand, lying 1,600 km (1,000 mi) southeast of Australia, consists mainly of two islands—the North Island and the South Island, separated by the narrow Cook Strait. North Island contains the capital, Wellington. New Zealand also has a number of small overseas territories in the Pacific Ocean, notably Tokelau, Niue, and the Cook Islands.

NATIONAL DATA – NEW ZEALAND

Land area 268,021 sq km (103,483 sq mi)

Climate	Altitude m (ft)	Temperatures January °C(°F)	July °C(°F)	Annual precipitation mm (in)
Wellington	126 (413)	18 (64)	9 (48)	1,018 (40)

Major physical features highest point: Mount Cook 3,764 m (12,349 ft); largest lake: Lake Taupo 606 sq km (234 sq mi)

Population (2006 est.) 4,177,937

Form of government multiparty constitutional monarchy with one legislative house

Armed forces army 4,430; navy 1,980; air force 2,250

Largest cities Auckland (1,442,101); Wellington (capital – 448,959); Christchurch (375,145); Hamilton (158,402); Napier (53,658); Dunedin (116,240); Tauranga (117,594)

Official languages English, Maori

Ethnic composition European 69.8%; Maori 7.9%; Asian 5.7%; Pacific islander 4.4%; other 0.5%; mixed 7.8%; unspecified 3.8%

Religious affiliations Anglican 14.9%; Roman Catholic 12.4%; Presbyterian 10.9%; Methodist 2.9%; Pentecostal 1.7%; Baptist 1.3%; other Christian 9.4%; other 3.3%; unspecified 17.2%; none 26%

Currency 1 New Zealand dollar (NZD) = 100 cents

Gross domestic product (2006) U.S. $106 billion

Gross domestic product per capita (2006) U.S. $26,000

Life expectancy at birth male 75.82 yr; female 81.93 yr

Major resources natural gas, iron ore, sand, coal, timber, hydropower, gold, limestone, cattle, cereals, fish, fruit, vegetables, sheep, tourism

Geography

The South Island is dominated by the great fold-mountain belt of the Southern Alps. The center contains the highest peaks, including Mount Cook and Mount Tasman. The Tasman Glacier flows down Mount Cook's eastern side. In the southwest, where the mountains meet the sea, the flooded valleys form steep fjords, creating Fiordland, New Zealand's largest national park. The only lowland areas on the South Island are scattered alluvial plains in the east. The mountains of the North Island are lower and more fragmented. In the

Sheep farming is the major economic activity in New Zealand, and lamb and wool are the chief exports. There are some 70 million sheep in the country.

central and eastern uplands there is considerable geothermal activity, with geysers, hot springs, and several active volcanoes. The hill slopes, river terraces, and scattered lowlands of the North Island provide some of the country's best agricultural land.

Wellington and Auckland are both built around large natural harbors. New Zealand has a mainly temperate maritime climate with regular rainfall all year. Summers are warm, except in the mountains, and winters are mild, particularly on the North Island, the warmer of the two islands. On the South Island the western mountains receive heavy rainfall, while sheltered eastern areas are often unusually dry.

Society

During the 19th and 20th centuries Britain had a powerful influence on New Zealand society, but today the people are keen to demonstrate their separate identity. The first settlers were people now known as Maori, who came from the Polynesian islands sometime between 800 and 1200. The first European to arrive was Dutch explorer Abel Janszoon Tasman (c.1603–59), followed in 1769 to 1770 by British Captain James Cook (1728–79). Later, Australian traders and whalers and British and French missionaries came to the islands. The Maoris ceded sovereignty to the British crown in 1840 in return for protection and land rights, and in 1841 New Zealand became a crown colony. The discovery of gold in the 1860s attracted many more immigrants. People born in New Zealand of European parents began to gain a greater sense of nationhood, and in 1907 the colony was granted dominion status within the British Empire. In both world wars New Zealanders fought alongside Britain and its allies, but after 1945 the country sought new alliances with the United States and some Southeast Asian countries.

Most New Zealanders are of original European descent—mainly British—but the Maori account for nearly 8 percent of people. Recently there has been an improvement in the legal and social status of the Maori, enabling them to recover some of their ancestral lands. Maori arts and crafts have also been revived, along with traditional forms of music and dance, and the Maori language has official status alongside English. Various

NEW ZEALAND'S UNIQUE WILDLIFE

Nine-tenths of the indigenous plants are unique to the islands, including kauri pines, southern beeches, and various ferns. Once, the only significantly sized animals, apart from birds, were two bat species and about 30 reptile species. Among the few native reptiles alive today is the tuatara, the sole survivor of a group that died out elsewhere 60 million years ago. In the absence of native mammalian predators, remarkable flightless birds developed—such as the kiwi and the kakapo, the world's largest parrot. Another large parrot, the kea, lives in the snow-covered Southern Alps.

smaller ethnic communities also exist. Cultural and leisure activities are European-based, and sport, especially rugby football, has a strong following.

Economy

In the first half of the 20th century New Zealand had one of the world's highest standards of living. But in the 1970s it experienced a loss of export trade with European Union countries, keen to protect their own markets. However, in the late 1980s and 1990s New Zealand successfully expanded its industrial and service sectors. Agriculture employs 9 percent of the workforce and supplies 8 percent of GDP. Sheep farming provides much of this, although cattle also provide exports of beef and butter. Cereals, vegetables, and fruit are exported. Forestry and fishing are important, with imported California Monterey pine producing timber and timber products such as woodchip and paper.

Industry is based around food processing and agricultural machinery. Industries such as chemicals and motor vehicle assembly rely on imports. Coal is used for power and exported (to Japan), and natural gas has become an important fuel. Hydroelectricity is also an important power source. Financial services and banking are also key contributors to the economy.

New Zealand has good road and railroad systems, and regular ferries operate between the islands. Local air services are also well developed. Healthcare and welfare standards are high, as are literacy levels.

SOLOMON ISLANDS

The Solomon Islands, so named because they were thought to contain gold and other riches worthy of the biblical king Solomon, lie in the western Pacific. The Solomons are essentially two parallel chains of volcanic islands running southeast from the island of Bougainville. Farther east is the Santa Cruz group. Several of the volcanic islands are active. The climate is hot and humid, and the region is prone to cyclones. Most of the land is covered by rain forest, harboring wildlife including many bird species and a unique lizard—the giant Solomon Island skink.

Melanesians first colonized the islands in about 2000 B.C. Following earlier Spanish settlements, British missionaries established a settlement in the 1870s. In 1893 Britain declared the Solomons a protectorate. Independence from Britain was only gained in 1978, and the Solomon Islands is now a member of the Commonwealth. The region saw bitter fighting between Japanese and U.S. forces in World War II. In 1999 to 2000 ethnic violence in Guadalcanal between indigenous islanders and Malaitan migrants resulted in an Australian-led peacekeeping force being sent to the islands to restore order in 2003.

Agriculture, forestry, and fishing are the chief exports. The islands have some bauxite and gold. Light manufacturing and food processing, exists alongside handicraft industries such as basket making.

Typical Solomon Islands village dwellings of wooden shacks nestling among the forest by the water's edge.

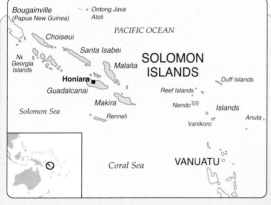

NATIONAL DATA – SOLOMON ISLANDS

Land area	27,540 sq km (10,633 sq mi)			
Climate	Altitude m (ft)	Temperatures		Annual precipitation mm (in)
		January °C(°F)	July °C(°F)	
Honiara	2 (7)	27 (80)	26 (79)	2,094 (82.4)

Major physical features largest island: Guadalcanal 5,336 sq km (2,060 sq mi); highest point: Makarakomburu 2,447 m (8,028 ft)
Population (2006 est.) 552,438
Form of government multiparty constitutional monarchy with one legislative house
Armed forces no armed forces
Capital city Honiara (Guadalcanal – 58,492)
Official language English
Ethnic composition Melanesian 94.5%; Polynesian 3%; Micronesian 1.2%; other 1.1%; unspecified 0.2%
Religious affiliations Church of Melanesia 32.8%; Roman Catholic 19%; South Seas Evangelical 17%; Seventh-Day Adventist 11.2%; United Church 10.3%; Christian Fellowship Church 2.4%; other Christian 4.4%; other 2.4%; unspecified 0.3%; none 0.2%
Currency 1 Solomon Islands dollar (SBD) = 100 cents
Gross domestic product (2005) U.S. $9.413 billion
Gross domestic product per capita (2005) U.S. $2,500
Life expectancy at birth male 70.4 yr; female 75.55 yr
Major resources fish, gold, bauxite, phosphates, lead, zinc, nickel, coconuts, livestock, palm kernels, rice, sweet potatoes, taro, timber

TUVALU

Tuvalu is a scattered island chain lying in the southwestern Pacific between the Gilbert Islands of Kiribati to the north and Fiji to the south. Tuvalu is made up of nine islands which are the peaks of an undersea mountain range. Five of the islands are coral atolls, and the other four are reef islands. They rise only a few yards above sea level, and rising sea levels and higher waves caused by global warming have damaged some coastal settlements. Furthermore, sea water has contaminated sources of fresh drinking water. The coral reefs have also been damaged by the crown-of-thorns starfish. The islands have a humid, tropical climate cooled by trade winds. Rainfall is often high, although severe droughts can occur. The poor soil supports only coconut palms, breadfruit, and cassowary trees. Wildlife includes rats, lizards, and seabirds, and the surrounding seas are rich in marine life.

The islands were probably first settled by seafaring Polynesians around the 14th century. In 1892 the British persuaded the islanders to join the Gilbert Islands protectorate, later the Gilbert and Ellice Islands. In 1976 the Ellice Islanders seceded, and the islands became independent as Tuvalu in 1978, but remain in the Commonwealth. Tuvalu's economy is based mainly on subsistence agriculture and fishing. Copra is the only cash crop. Fishing is mostly for the local market, except for sea cucumbers (a kind of marine animal), which are processed and exported. Many islanders find work abroad. In 2000, leasing the Internet domain name "tv" boosted Tuvalu's fortunes to the tune of $50 million.

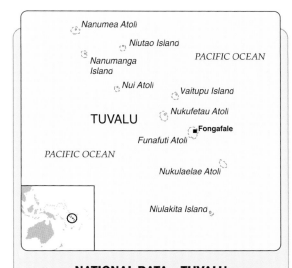

NATIONAL DATA – TUVALU

Land area	26 sq km (10 sq mi)			

Climate		Temperatures		Annual precipitation
	Altitude m (ft)	January °C(°F)	July °C(°F)	mm (in)
Funafuti atoll	2 (7)	28 (82)	28 (82)	3,544 (139.5)

Major physical features	largest island: Vaitupu 5 sq km (2 sq mi)

Population	(2006 est.) 11,810

Form of government	nonparty constitutional monarchy with one legislative house

Armed forces	no armed forces

Capital city	Fongafale (Funafuti, 4,921)

Official languages	Tuvaluan, English

Ethnic composition	Polynesian 96%; Micronesian 4%

Religious affiliations	Church of Tuvalu (Congregationalist) 97%; Seventh-Day Adventist 1.4%; Baha'i 1%; other 0.6%

Currency	1 Australian dollar (AUD) or 1 Tuvaluan dollar = 100 cents

Gross domestic product	(2002) U.S. $14.94 million

Gross domestic product per capita	(2002) U.S. $1,600

Life expectancy at birth	male 66.08 yr; female 70.66 yr

Major resources	fish, bananas, breadfruit, coconuts, copra, fish, papaya, root crops

NAURU

At only 21 sq km (8 sq mi), Nauru is the smallest republic in the world. It is situated in the western Pacific Ocean, immediately south of the equator and about 700 km (450 mi) west of Kiribati. The island is a raised coral reef with a central plateau, where rich phosphate beds have been created by bird droppings. The climate is hot and humid, although moderated by sea breezes. Rainfall is heavy during the monsoon season, but droughts can also occur. Vegetation consists mainly of coconut palms, breadfruit trees, and scrub. The precise origins of the Nauruans are unclear. The British discovered the island in 1798, and Germany annexed it in 1888. Australia occupied it in 1914, and it was brutally occupied by the Japanese in 1942 during World War II. The island was retaken by Australia in 1945 and became a UN trust territory. Nauru has been independent since 1968, joining the UN in 1999.

A strip of fertile land exists between the coast and the central plateau; coconuts, bananas, and pineapples are the main export crops. However, Nauru's prosperity comes mainly from its deposits of phosphates, which countries such as Japan, South Korea, New Zealand, and Australia use as fertilizer. Attempts to provide new revenue sources when the phosphate runs out (by 2008) have not been as successful as hoped, and although Nauru has a small offshore banking center, unwise overseas investments have reduced the nation almost to bankruptcy, and living standards have fallen.

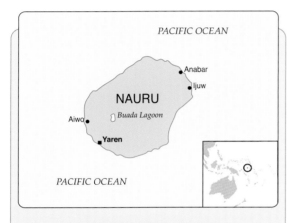

NATIONAL DATA – NAURU

Land area	21 sq km (8 sq mi)			
Climate		Temperatures		Annual
	Altitude m (ft)	January °C(°F)	July °C(°F)	precipitation mm (in)
Nauru	27 (89)	28 (82)	28 (82)	2,051 (80.8)

Major physical features	highest point: 69 m (225 ft)
Population	(2006 est.) 13,287
Form of government	nonparty republic with one legislative house
Armed forces	no armed forces
Capital city	No official capital but Yaren is the government seat (4,616)
Official languages	Nauruan, English
Ethnic composition	Nauruan 58%; other Pacific Islander 26%; Chinese 8%; European 8%
Religious affiliations	Christian 100% (two-thirds Protestant, one-third Roman Catholic)
Currency	1 Australian dollar (AUD) = 100 cents
Gross domestic product	(2005) U.S. $60 million
Gross domestic product per capita	(2005) U.S. $5,000
Life expectancy at birth	male 59.5 yr; female 66.84 yr
Major resources	phosphates, fish, bananas, coconuts, pineapples

KIRIBATI

Kiribati's flag, a frigatebird flying over a sun-kissed azure sea, is a fitting symbol for the republic. It consists of three archipelagos scattered across a vast area of the central Pacific Ocean. The largest of these island groups are the Gilbert Islands, the Phoenix Islands, and the Line Islands. The islands are coral atolls—essentially the tops of undersea volcanoes encircled by reefs. They only rise a yard or so above sea level. The climate of Kiribati is hot and humid, with rainfall regular in the Gilberts but sparser and generally unreliable elsewhere. The soil is poor, and vegetation is mostly salt-resistant plants and palms—mainly coconuts and bananas. However, the surrounding seas are rich in marine life, providing the islanders with much of their food.

The Gilbert Islands were settled several thousand years ago by Micronesian peoples. In 1900 the British annexed Banaba Island for its phosphates and forcibly resettled its population. In 1916 the Gilbert and Ellice

Kiribati's blue waters and palm-fringed coral beaches have captivated visitors for centuries. Only the Gilberts and three of the Line Islands are now inhabited.

Islands colony was founded, later to include the Phoenix and Line Islands. In 1978 the Ellice Islands gained independence as Tuvalu, and in 1979 the remaining colony became independent as Kiribati. Phosphate deposits on Banaba were exhausted in the late 1970s, and now Kiribati's income is derived from subsistence farming and remittances from islanders working abroad. Foreign aid accounts for up to half of GDP.

NATIONAL DATA – KIRIBATI

Land area   811 sq km (313 sq mi)

Climate		Temperatures		Annual
	Altitude m (ft)	January °C(°F)	July °C(°F)	precipitation mm (in)
Tarawa	3 (10)	28 (82)	28 (82)	1,914 (75.4)

Major physical features   largest island: Kiritmati (Line Is) 388 sq km (150 sq mi); highest point: Banaba 81 m (266 ft)

Population   (2006 est.) 105,432

Form of government   multiparty republic with one legislative house

Armed forces   no armed forces

Capital city   Tarawa (47,437)

Official language   English

Ethnic composition   Micronesian 98.8%; other 1.2%

Religious affiliations   Roman Catholic 52%; Protestant (Congregational) 40%; Seventh-Day Adventist, Muslim, Baha'i, Latter-day Saints, Church of God 8%

Currency   1 Australian dollar (AUD) = 100 cents

Gross domestic product   (2004) U.S. $206.4 million

Gross domestic product per capita   (2004) U.S. $2,700

Life expectancy at birth   male 59.06 yr; female 65.24 yr

Major resources   bananas, breadfruit, coconuts, copra, fish, papaya

Fiji is an isolated archipelago located in the southwestern Pacific, about 2,100 km (1,300 mi) north of Auckland, New Zealand. There are about 320 islands in the group, together with another 480 or so islets, but only about 110 are inhabited. Most of the islands are tiny, and the two largest—Viti Levu and Vanua Levu—account for almost nine-tenths of the total land area.

NATIONAL DATA – FIJI

Land area	18,270 sq km (7,054 sq mi)			
Climate		Temperatures		Annual precipitation
	Altitude m (ft)	January °C(°F)	July °C(°F)	mm (in)
Suva	6 (20)	27 (80)	23 (73)	3.040 (119.6)

Major physical features largest island: Viti Levu 10,386 sq km (4,010 sq mi); highest point: Mount Tomanivi (on Vitu Levu) 1,323 m (4,341 ft)

Population (2006 est.) 905,949

Form of government multiparty republic with two legislative houses

Armed forces army 3,200; navy 300

Capital city Suva (206,631)

Official language English

Ethnic composition Fijian 51% (mainly Melanesian with a Polynesian admixture); Indian 44%; European, other Pacific Islanders, overseas Chinese, and other 5%

Religious affiliations Christian 52% (Methodist 37%; Roman Catholic 9%); Hindu 38%; Muslim 8%; other 2%

Currency 1 Fijian dollar (FJD) = 100 cents

Gross domestic product (2006) U.S. $5.504 billion

Gross domestic product per capita (2006) U.S. $6,100

Life expectancy at birth male 67.32 yr; female 72.45 yr

Major resources timber, fish, gold, copper, offshore oil potential, hydropower, bananas, cassava, cocoa, coconuts, ginger, livestock, rice, sugarcane, sweet potatoes, tobacco, tourism

Geography

As is the case with most of the Fijian islands, Viti Levu and Vanua Levu are volcanic in origin, with dramatic central mountain ranges rising abruptly from narrow coastal plains and offshore coral reefs. The tropical climate brings hot and humid conditions from November to April, with the danger of cyclones. The southeastern coastline, facing the southeast trade winds, is clad in tropical rain forest and receives heavy rainfall. The western slopes have vegetation of grassy plains and open forests with clumps of palmlike pandanus trees. Here conditions are much drier. Although about two-thirds of the land area of Fiji is forested, some of the hillsides have been deforested to create grazing, which is now causing soil erosion. Viti Levu is the site of the capital, Suva, and is home to almost three-quarters of the population. The international airport is located at Nadi. The major towns on Vanua Levu are Labasa and Savusavu.

Fiji's beautiful coral beaches have helped the country develop a flourishing and vitally important tourist trade.

History

When the Dutch explorer and navigator Abel Janszoon Tasman (c.1603–59) arrived on Fiji in 1643, the inhabitants were a mixture of Polynesian and Melanesian peoples. It was not until the 19th century that Europeans settled in the islands permanently. The islands became a British crown colony in 1874, and the British imported thousands of Indian laborers to work their sugar plantations. Fiji was granted independence in 1970. However, the political parties divided along racial lines, creating considerable political instability. After the election in 1987 there were concerns that the government was perceived as being too dominated by the Indo-Fijian community (descendants of the labor force brought to the islands by the British). This concern led to two military coups, and as a result there was

heavy Indian emigration coupled with an economic downturn. A constitution of 1990 confirmed ethnic Fijian control of the country, and later amendments made it fairer for all. Free and open elections were held in 1999, bringing in a government headed by an Indo-Fijian. Since then there has been a succession of either civilian or military coups (with one late in 2006), alternating with rule by civilian governments.

Economy

Fiji is well endowed with natural resources of timber, minerals such as gold, fish in the seas around the coasts, and a natural beauty. The economy is one of the best developed among Pacific island nations, although it still relies on a large degree of subsistence. The economy suffered badly during the years of unrest, however, and agriculture, tourism, and light industry are striving to gain lost ground. Major cash crops are sugarcane, copra, ginger, and coconuts. Fiji's sugarcane industry—the processing of which makes up one-third of industrial activity—has special access to the markets of the EU, although this will be harmed by the EU's decision to cut sugar subsidies. Gold, another important export, is mined on Viti Levu. Also vital to the economy are the remittances sent home from Fijians working abroad, especially in the Middle East. Tourism has attracted about 400,000 tourists a year in the past and has the potential to be a major industry, but its success depends on the internal tensions being resolved.

THE RUGBY-PLAYING FIJIANS

To the great Southern Hemisphere rugby-playing nations—New Zealand, South Africa, Australia, and Argentina—must be added the name of Fiji. This tiny nation embraced the sport of rugby union as far back as the 1880s, and the game is now part of Fijian culture. Fijians are skilled players, tackling hard and running with the ball at speed and with purpose. Since 1987 the national team has competed at four world cups, reaching the quarter finals once. The rugby sevens team is also noted for its success and has won world championships in this form of the game.

VANUATU

Vanuatu lies in the southwestern Pacific. Formerly the New Hebrides (before independence in 1980), it comprises 13 main islands and many smaller ones, forming a Y-shaped group between the Solomon Islands to the north and New Caledonia to the south. The principal islands are Espiritu Santo and Efaté. Most of the islands, including these two, are mountainous and covered in rain forest, with raised coral terraces on some coastal slopes and offshore coral reefs. Earth tremors often occur, and there are several active volcanoes. The humid tropical climate can produce cyclones.

Melanesians lived here for more than 2,500 years before European settlers first arrived in the 15th century. Vanuatu's economy is based largely on exports of copra, fish, beef, and veal. Most manufactured goods and fuel need to be imported. About three-quarters of the workforce is engaged in agriculture, mostly as subsistence farmers raising livestock and crops such as bananas and yams. Other exports include manganese, which is mined on Efaté, and timber. Tourism is a growing source of foreign currency, and Vanuatu's tax laws have helped it develop as a financial center.

A native Polynesian fishing canoe, complete with outrigger, drawn up on a remote beach on an island in Tonga.

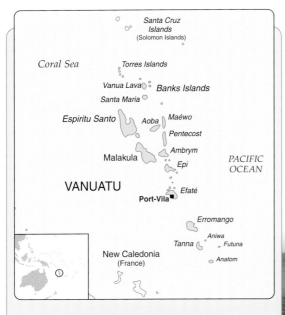

NATIONAL DATA – VANUATU

Land area	12,200 sq km (4,710 sq mi)			

Climate		Temperatures		Annual
	Altitude m (ft)	January °C(°F)	July °C(°F)	precipitation mm (in)
Port-Vila	57 (187)	27 (81)	23 (73)	2,221 (87.4)

Major physical features highest point: Espiritu Santo 3,678 sq km (1,420 sq mi); highest point: Tabwémanasana on Espiritu Santo 1,880 m (6,167 ft)

Population (2006 est.) 208,869

Form of government multiparty republic with one legislative house

Armed forces no armed forces

Capital city Port-Vila (38,438)

Official languages French, English

Ethnic composition Ni-Vanuatu 98.5%; other 1.5%

Religious affiliations Presbyterian 31.4%; Anglican 13.4%; Roman Catholic 13.1%; Seventh-Day Adventist 10.8%; other Christian 13.8%; traditional beliefs 5.6% (including Jon Frum cargo cult); other 9.6%; none 1%; unspecified 1.3%

Currency vatu (VUV)

Gross domestic product (2003) U.S. $276.3 million

Gross domestic product per capita (2003) U.S. $2,900

Life expectancy at birth male 61.34 yr; female 64.44 yr

Major resources manganese, hardwood forests, fish, bananas, cassava, cattle, cocoa, coconuts, coffee, taro, yams, tourism

TONGA

Tonga, lying in the Pacific Ocean to the southwest of Samoa and east of Fiji, is a double chain of 169 islands. From north to south the islands are in three main groups: Vava'u, Ha'apai, and Tongatapu. The Vava'u islands and one island in the Ha'apai group consist of mountainous volcanic rock, and there are four intermittently active volcanoes. The rest of the islands are lowlying coral formations. The climate is semitropical and encourages a rich variety of mainly forest vegetation, including species such as mulberry. The islands have varied birdlife, and some of the world's largest bats—the flying foxes—are also found there.

The settlement of Tonga started in about 1000 B.C., and since the 10th century A.D. kingship has been handed down from the original Tu'i Tonga royal line. In 1875 the king of Tonga created a constitutional monarchy, and this system of government has continued virtually unchanged ever since. In 1970 Tonga regained

independence within the Commonwealth. Agriculture is the mainstay of the economy; cash crops include vanilla, coconuts, and bananas. Traditional handicrafts cater to the growing tourist market, but remittances sent home by Tongans working abroad also help the economy.

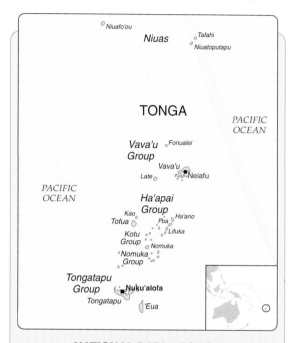

NATIONAL DATA – TONGA

Land area	718 sq km (277 sq mi)			

Climate		Temperatures		Annual
	Altitude m (ft)	January °C(°F)	July °C(°F)	precipitation mm (in)
Nuku'alofa	3 (10)	26 (78)	21 (70)	1,738 (68.4)

Major physical features highest point: Tongatapu 256 sq km (99 sq mi); highest point: on Kao Island 1,030 m (3,380 ft)

Population (2006 est.) 114,689

Form of government nonparty constitutional monarchy with one legislative house

Armed forces no armed forces

Capital city Nuku'alofa (23,854)

Official languages Tongan, English

Ethnic composition Tongan 96%; Part-Tongan 1.7%; European 0.6%; Fijian 0.2%; Samoan 0.2%; Indian, Chinese, Japanese 0.3%; Other 1%

Religious affiliations Christian 100% (Free Wesleyan Church claims over 30,000 adherents)

Currency 1 pa'anga (TOP) = 100 seniti

Gross domestic product (2004) U.S. $178.5 million

Gross domestic product per capita (2005) U.S. $2,200

Life expectancy at birth male 67.32 yr; female 72.45 yr

Major resources fish, bananas, cassava, citrus fruits, coconuts, sweet potatoes, taro, vanilla, tourism

SAMOA

Samoa consists of nine islands lying in the south-central Pacific Ocean to the north of Tonga and northeast of Fiji. Upolu, Savai'i, Apolima, and Manono are the only inhabited islands. Upolu and Savai'i—the largest islands—have mountainous interiors, with coral reefs ringing the narrow coastal plains. All the islands are volcanic. The climate is warm and humid, with heavy rainfall on the southeastern slopes facing the trade winds. Nearly half the land is covered with forest, and mangroves grow in the lowland swamps. Wildlife is sparse but includes the rare tooth-billed pigeon.

The islands were probably settled by Tongans in about 1000 B.C., and the first European visitor was the French explorer Bougainville (1729–1811). Later, Britain, Germany, and the United States all had colonial interests there. The islands achieved independence in 1962 as Western Samoa, changing the name to Samoa in 1977.

The chief economic activities are agriculture, fishing, lumber, and tourism. Copra and coca are grown as cash crops, and yams, breadfruit, and papaya are grown for local consumption. The country relies mainly on hydroelectricity for power. Light industries are growing, and handicrafts meet the demands of the tourist trade. Nevertheless, many economically active Samoans have emigrated to New Zealand, which has restricted further development, even though the country's stability encourages foreign investors.

Open-sided thatched houses, such as this one erected on a coral beach, are the traditional dwelling for many Samoans.

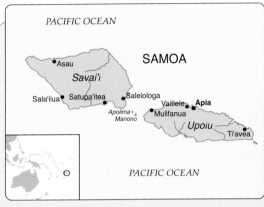

NATIONAL DATA – SAMOA

Land area	2,934 sq km (1,133 sq mi)			

Climate		Temperatures		Annual
	Altitude m (ft)	January °C(°F)	July °C(°F)	precipitation mm (in)
Apia	2 (7)	27 (72)	26 (79)	2,961 (116.5)

Major physical features largest island: Savai'i 1,813 sq km (700 sq mi); highest point: Silsili (Savai'i) 1,858 m (6,095 ft)

Population (2006 est.) 176,908

Form of government multiparty republic with two legislative houses

Armed forces no armed forces

Capital city Apia (41,204)

Official languages Samoan, English

Ethnic composition Samoan 92.6%; Euronesians 7% (persons of European and Polynesian blood); Europeans 0.4%

Religious affiliations Congregationalist 34.8%; Roman Catholic 19.6%; Methodist 15%; Latter-Day Saints 12.7%; Assembly of God 6.6%; Seventh-Day Adventist 3.5%; other Christian 4.5%; Worship Centre 1.3%; other 1.7%; unspecified 0.1%

Currency 1 tala (SAT) = 100 seniti

Gross domestic product (2002) U.S. $1 billion

Gross domestic product per capita (2005) U.S. $2,100

Life expectancy at birth male 68.2 yr; female 73.94 yr

Major resources hardwood forests, fish, hydropower, bananas, coffee, copra, tropical fruits, tourism

PALAU

Palau, or Belau, comprises the westernmost part of the Caroline Islands chain about 850 km (528 mi) southeast of the Philippines. The main islands consist of a coralline reef structure on top of a volcanic base, with more than 300 islets surrounding a large central lagoon. The islands vary in their geological structure: the main island, Babelthuap, is mountainous, with coastal plains surrounding a wooded interior; the new capital, Melekeok, is being built on this island. Other islands are lowlying and fringed by barrier reefs.

The reefs are home to a wide variety of marine life, including colorful anemones, mollusks, corals, and numerous reef fish species ranging from snappers and bonito to tuna and sharks. Other marine life includes sea snakes, dugongs, and crocodiles. This rich collection of animals attracts tourists who dive to view the marine life in its natural habitat. However, the waters off Palau are also the resting place for some reminders of a more troubled time in the islands' history. The rusting remains of gray warships, bombers, and fighter aircraft haunt the reefs and lagoons of Palau's crystal waters, for this

region saw some of the heaviest fighting during World War II. More than 15,000 men died in 10 weeks of fierce battles between Japanese and U.S. forces attempting to gain control of this strategic location between the Pacific and Indian Oceans.

Palau became independent in 1994, having been a UN trusteeship in free association with the United States. Agriculture and fishing remain at subsistence level, although tuna is exported, and copra is raised as a cash crop. Coconut oil is exported in small amounts. The tourist industry has not yet been fully developed.

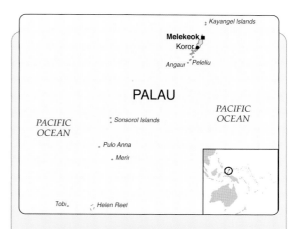

NATIONAL DATA – PALAU

Land area   458 sq km (177 sq mi)

Major physical features   26 islands and over 300 islets; largest island is Babelthuap

Population   (2006 est.) 20,579

Form of government   constitutional republic with two legislative houses

Armed forces   no armed forces

Capital city   Melekeok (391) replaced Koror (11,559) in 2006

Official languages   Palauan and English are official in all islands except Sonsoral (Sonsoralese and English are official), Tobi (Tobi and English are official), and Angaur (Angaur, Japanese, and English are official)

Ethnic composition   Palauan (Micronesian with Malayan and Melanesian admixtures) 69.9%; Filipino 15.3%; Chinese 4.9%; other Asian 2.4%; white 1.9%; Carolinian 1.4%; other Micronesian 1.1%; other or unspecified 3.2%

Religious affiliations   Roman Catholic 41.6%; Protestant 23.3%; Modekngei 8.8% (indigenous to Palau); Seventh-Day Adventist 5.3%; Jehovah's Witness 0.9%; Latter-Day Saints 0.6%; other religion 3.1%; unspecified or none 16.4%

Currency   1 U.S. dollar (USD) = 100 cents

Gross domestic product   (2004) U.S. $124.5 million

Gross domestic product per capita   (2005) U.S. $7,600

Life expectancy at birth   male 67.26 yr; female 73.77 yr

Major resources   forests, gold, marine products, deep-seabed minerals, fish, root crops, copra, coconuts, tourism

MARSHALL ISLANDS

The Marshall Islands are a collection of five islands, 31 widely scattered coral atolls (including the world's largest atoll), and more than 1,000 islets and reefs running northwest to southeast in two chains in the western Pacific Ocean. They were named for John Marshall (1748–1819), a British mariner who visited the islands in 1788. During World War II the islands were occupied by the Allied forces, and from 1949 they became part of the Trust Territory of the United States. In 1986 the Marshall Islands became self-governing in free association with the United States—an arrangement whereby the latter retains responsibility for defense in return for assistance. Bikini Atoll and Enewetak Atoll are famous among the islands as being the site where more than 60 nuclear weapon test explosions were carried out by the United States between 1946 and 1958.

Local politics are traditionally dominated by the island chiefs, with their high chief holding the position of president. Typically, islanders live in simple houses constructed from woven mats and roofed with coconut palm fronds. The islands' economy is still heavily dependent on U.S. aid, and the rent paid by its benefactor for the use of Kwajalein Atoll—the largest of the atolls—as a missile base. The tourist industry is an important form of revenue and employment. High-quality phosphate is mined on Ailinglapalap Atoll, although most of the other industries are limited to handicrafts and the processing of fish and copra. Agriculture is carried out mostly at subsistence level, but a few cash crops—such as coconuts, tomatoes, melons, and breadfruit—are grown in small amounts.

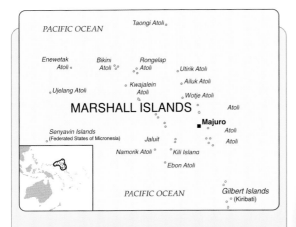

NATIONAL DATA – MARSHALL ISLANDS

Land area   181 sq km (70 sq mi)

Climate	Altitude m (ft)	Temperatures January °C(°F)	July °C(°F)	Annual precipitation mm (in)
Ujelang Atoll	10 (33)	27 (81)	28 (82)	1,976 (77.8)

Population   (2006 est.) 60,422

Form of government   Constitutional government in free association with the United States of America

Armed forces   no armed forces

Capital city   Majuro (25,400)

Official language   English

Ethnic composition   Micronesian 100%

Religious affiliations   Protestant 54.8%; Assembly of God 25.8%; Roman Catholic 8.4%; Bukot nan Jesus 2.8%; Mormon 2.1%; other Christian 3.6%; other 1%; none 1.5%

Currency   1 U.S. dollar (USD) = 100 cents

Gross domestic product   (2001) U.S. $115 million

Gross domestic product per capita   (2005) U.S. $2,900

Life expectancy at birth   male 68.33 yr; female 72.39 yr

Major resources   coconuts, copra, fruits, deep-seabed minerals, phosphates, clams, fish, livestock, oysters, tourism

MICRONESIA

Scattered across a huge expanse of the western Pacific Ocean to the north of Papua New Guinea, the Federated States of Micronesia are a group of 600 or so volcanic islands and atolls including the eastern and central Caroline Islands. The islands have lush tropical vegetation and extensive rain forest. The islands of Micronesia stretch more than 3,200 km (2,000 mi) from end to end, yet together only make up an area of just over 700 sq km (about 271 sq mi). The island of Pohnpei, on which the capital, Palikir, is located, accounts for almost half the total land area.

Various colonists have laid claim to the islands, including Spain (who gave the Caroline Islands their name), Germany, and Japan. There then followed U.S. rule as part of the Trust Territory of the Pacific Islands; this effectively gave self-government to the islands, while at the same time safeguarding U.S. defense

One of the 600 islands that make up the Federated States of Micronesia. The hot, rainy climate encourages lush vegetation.

interests in the area. In 1986 the islands were released from a UN trusteeship administered by the United States, and in 1991 they gained full independence.

The inhabitants of the larger towns have adopted a somewhat Americanized way of life, but for many elsewhere life is much as it was before centuries of colonial rule. The main economic activities are subsistence farming and fishing, although a small quantity of cash crops—copra, bananas, citrus fruits, peppers, and taro—are grown for export. The islands once depended heavily on U.S. aid, grants, and military spending, but they intend to develop tourism and generate income from selling fishing rights and crops.

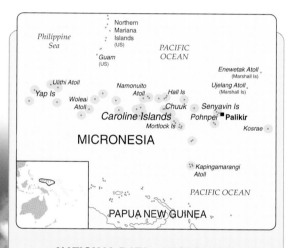

NATIONAL DATA - MICRONESIA

Land area 702 sq km (271 sq mi)

Climate	Altitude m (ft)	Temperatures January °C(°F)	July °C(°F)	Annual precipitation mm (in)
Palikir	0 (0)	27 (81)	27 (81)	4,907 (193.2)

Population (2006 est.) 108,004

Form of government federal republic

Capital city Palikir (on the island of Pohnpei, 4,462)

Official language English

Ethnic composition Chuukese/Mortlockese 49%; Pohnpeian 24%; Kosraean 6%; Yapese 5%; Yap Outer Islands 5%; Polynesian 1%; Asian 2%; White 1%; Others 7%

Religious affiliations Roman Catholic 50%; Protestant 47%; other 3%

Currency 1 U.S. dollar (USD) = 100 cents

Gross domestic product (2002) U.S. $277 million

Gross domestic product per capita (2005) U.S. $2,300

Life expectancy at birth male 68.24 yr; female 71.95 yr

Major resources forests, marine products, deep-seabed minerals, phosphates, tourism, bananas, citrus fruits, copra, peppers, taro, fish, livestock

ANTARCTICA

The ice-covered continent of Antarctica has a land area bigger than Europe or the United States and Mexico combined. This frozen but fragile region, Earth's most southerly landmass, has attracted explorers and adventurers for more than 200 years. Antarctica is the world's coldest continent. The harsh climate has prevented any large-scale settlements, and although hunters built outposts in the past, scientific bases are today the only permanent form of human habitation.

Geography

About 95 percent of Antarctica is covered by an ice cap formed by thousands of years of accumulated snow which is 4,000 m (13,000 ft) deep in places—nine-tenths of the world's glacial ice is held here. At an average height of 2,000 m (7,000 ft) above sea level, it is the world's highest continent. In high winter (August to September), pack ice up to 3 m (10 ft) deep extends over the surrounding Southern Ocean, doubling the size of the continent.

The Transantarctic Mountains run across the whole of the continent, passing near the South Pole and dividing Antarctica into two unequal halves: Lesser Antarctica, lying mostly within western longitudes, and the broadly semicircular mass of Greater Antarctica. From Lesser Antarctica the Antarctic Peninsula stretches north to form the western boundary of the Weddell Sea. The Ross Sea forms a smaller gulf on the opposite side of Lesser Antarctica. Toward the land, the Ross Ice Shelf contains over 30 percent of all Antarctic ice.

Other mountain ranges occur on the edges of the ice cap, the highest being the Vinson Massif (4,897 m/ 16,067 ft) in Lesser Antarctica. Volcanoes are present, including the active Mount Erebus on Ross Island. Temperatures in August can drop to –95°F (–70°C) on the inland ice sheet. On the Antarctic Peninsula milder winds raise temperatures to 59°F (15°C), but elsewhere Antarctica is bitterly cold all year. Rainfall is rare, and snowfall is scarce except at the coast, but fierce winds can whip the snow into blizzards. The cold conditions and long months of darkness limit plant life to lichens, mosses, algae, and molds. No land mammals are found on Antarctica, but the seas support seals and whales. Birdlife is rich and includes penguins, skuas, and petrels.

History

The Maoris claim the first sighting of the icebound Southern Ocean, but the first European to cross the Antarctic Circle, in 1773, was British Captain James Cook (1728–79). Members of Russian, British, and U.S. expeditions first sighted the mainland in 1820. Parts of Antarctica were charted by later expeditions, including one led by James Ross Clark (1800–62), who discovered the sea and ice shelf that bear his name. Early in the

1959 sovereign claims have been largely ignored, and scientists from many countries work together.

Antarctic Research

Earlier explorers on the continent had to battle against the bitter elements using rudimentary equipment and traveling on sleds hauled by dog teams. But today's explorers wear hi-tech clothing and travel in adapted vehicles known as snow cats. They live in specially constructed bases that are supplied with everything required for life in this harsh terrain. They use sophisticated seismic and remote-sensing equipment to map the contours of the hidden continent buried beneath the ice. Other research includes planetary geology, hydrology, and meteoritics.

In 1981 scientists discovered that there was massive damage to the ozone layer above the South Pole, and in 1988 they had traced the cause to the use of chlorofluorocarbons (CFCs) in aerosols, packaging, and refrigerants. More recently, studies such as monitoring the reduction in size of the Ross Ice Shelf are providing scientists with information about the possible effects of global warming. Apart from reserving the continent for nonpolitical scientific exploration, the 1959 Antarctic Treaty also imposed restrictions on the hunting of seals and whales, but fishing in Antarctic waters has increased. Since the 1950s a small but significant tourist industry has existed. Visits by cruise ships are strictly controlled, to minimize environmental damage.

ANTARCTICA'S MINERAL RICHES

Geological surveys have revealed the presence of many minerals in Antarctica. The Transantarctic Mountains have possibly the world's largest reserves of coal, and there are sizeable quantities of iron ore in the Prince Charles Mountains near the coast of Greater Antarctica. Other minerals such as antimony, chromium, gold, uranium, and molybdenum have also been discovered. At present, however, it would not be economically viable to extract any minerals, and such activity would damage the environment. In 1990 it was agreed internationally to ban mining and mineral exploitation for 50 years.

Many of the world's penguin species are found in Antarctica, where they hunt in the ocean for fish and other marine life.

20th century several expeditions set out to reach the South Pole at the heart of Antarctica. The first to arrive was that of Roald Amundsen in 1911. By 1942 seven nations—Chile, Australia, France, Norway, Argentina, New Zealand, and Britain—had laid claim to different parts of the Antarctic, but since the Antarctic Treaty of

AMERICAN SAMOA

Unincorporated Organized Territory of the United States

American Samoa consists of five islands and two atolls situated along the east coast of the Samoan archipelago in the south-central Pacific Ocean about 2,600 km (1,600 mi) northeast of New Zealand. The largest island, Tutuila, accounts for over two-thirds of the total land area. Pago Pago on Tutuila has one of the best natural deepwater harbors in the South Pacific Ocean. The climate is hot and humid, punctuated by occasional violent cyclones.

Every Samoan belongs to an extended family headed by a chief. Families live in villages, each controlled by a council of chiefs according to ancient custom; the chiefs' councils elect the Senate within the national assembly. The population of American Samoa is about 58,000. Tuna canning and tourism are the main industries. Canned tuna—sold mostly to the United States—accounts for almost all of the country's export revenue. The United States also supplies aid. Standard of living and educational facilities are good.

Cook Islanders dancing. Tourism is mostly confined to Rarotonga, which has an international airport.

COOK ISLANDS

Self-governing State in Free Association with New Zealand

On his second Pacific voyage in 1773, Captain James Cook (1728–79) discovered many of the islands that today bear his name. The Cook Islands consist of 15 small islands scattered over a vast area (about 2.2 million sq km (850,00 sq mi) of the Pacific Ocean to the east of Tonga, approximately midway between Australia and South America. The islands lie in two main groups about 1,100 km (700 mi) apart. The northern group is composed of six coral islands. The southern group is mostly volcanic and contains 90 percent of the total land area. It includes Rarotonga, the largest of the islands and also the most mountainous—Te Manga reaches a height of 652 m (2,139 ft). The majority of the population lives on the nine southern islands, which have the most fertile soils.

In 1888 the Cook Islands became a British protectorate but passed to New Zealand in 1901. In 1965 they gained independence in free association with New Zealand. Defense and foreign affairs are handled by New Zealand. The islands are also a member of the Commonwealth. The population of about 21,000 is outnumbered by the number of Cook Islanders who work abroad—almost entirely in New Zealand—and send remittances home to help the economy. The main economic activity of the islands is agriculture, with produce mainly exported to New Zealand. Black pearls are the major export commodity. The northern islands provide coconuts as the main crop, while the more fertile south islands grow citrus fruits, pineapples, bananas, and tomatoes. A limited export market, few resources, and a weak infrastructure mean that the islands also rely on foreign aid from New Zealand.

FRENCH POLYNESIA

Overseas Territory of France

Perhaps the archetypal South Sea paradise, French Polynesia consists of five archipelagos scattered over 4 million sq km (1.5 million sq mi) of the south-central Pacific Ocean. The islands—about 130 or so in total—include low coral atolls and reefs, as well as a number of larger volcanic cone-shaped islands covered in lush

Bora-Bora, in the Leeward group of islands (part of the islands that make up French Polynesia), is surrounded by a lagoon and reef.

vegetation. There are five main island groups. The Windward Islands and the Leeward Islands together form the Society group. These islands and the Marquesas, plus the majority of the Tubuais and the Gambier Islands, are volcanic in origin and have steep mountains. The Tuamotus are lowlying atolls, however.

The islands were first inhabited by Polynesians who settled from the Marquesas southward during the 5th century A.D. In 1840 the islands became a French colony and in 1946 an overseas territory. Although there have been calls for full independence, it is feared that a loss of revenue from the French government in the form of military expenditure would result. One of the best-known islands is Tahiti in the Society group. It is an expanding tourist center and home to more than two-thirds of the population. Most of the islanders are Polynesians, but there is a large French community as well as a Chinese one. French is the official language, but many people also speak Tahitian.

Phosphate mining was once important, but it ceased in the 1960s. Light industry is mainly centered on the processing of agricultural products. A high proportion of the workforce (about 68 percent) is employed either in a military capacity or in the tourist industry—about one-quarter of GDP comes from tourism.

The Administration Buildings on Norfolk Island, part of the historic colonial heritage of this tourist destination.

GUAM
Unincorporated Organized Territory of the United States

Guam is the largest and the most southerly of the Mariana Islands. Situated about 2,250 km (1,400 mi) southeast of Okinawa in Japan, the island covers an area of about 549 sq km (212 sq mi). Micronesian peoples inhabited the island for 3,000 years before it was discovered by Ferdinand Magellan (1480–1521) in 1521, and later claimed for Spain. Following the Spanish–American War of 1898 Guam became an American territory, and it has remained so except during World War II, when it was held by the Japanese for several years. Guam has a landscape ranging from a thickly forested limestone plateau in the north of the island to low, grass-covered volcanic hills in the southwest. The densely forested nature of the island was highlighted in 1972 when it was discovered that a Japanese soldier had been hiding in the forests since the war, unaware that hostilities had long since ceased.

There are some attractive beaches on the island, which are important for the growing tourist industry as well as architectural reminders of Spanish rule. The climate is warm and wet but subject to the occasional violent typhoon. The population is Chamorro, of mixed descent—mainly Indonesian, Filipino, and Spanish. The economy is heavily dependent on the presence of the U.S. military, which has used Guam as a strategic base since World War II. The U.S. presence has ensured the island enjoys a higher standard of living than many other Micronesian islands. Most food and consumer goods are imported. Tourism is the second most valuable currency earner, with many visitors from Japan.

NEW CALEDONIA
Overseas Territory of France

The islands of New Caledonia, France's largest overseas territory, lie in the southwestern Pacific Ocean about 1,770 km (1,110 mi) north of New Zealand. The territory consists of one large hilly island and several smaller ones. The climate is warm and humid, supporting lush rain forests on the eastern slopes of the main islands. On the more sheltered western side the vegetation is open forests and savanna grasslands. The rainy season (December–March) may bring typhoons.

New Caledonia became a French possession in 1853 and served as a penal colony for four decades. A violent period arose during the 1980s and early 1990s as the territory pressed for independence. It resulted in

France agreeing to transfer an increasing amount of governing responsibility, leading to a series of referenda on whether or not full independence will be granted. New Caledonia has one of the world's largest deposits of nickel, and mining the ore accounts for 12 percent of national income. Tourism has become an important industry. Most people practice subsistence farming and fishing, but the territory relies on French aid. Health and education facilities are generally good and are concentrated in Noumea, the capital and main port.

NIUE
Self-governing State in Free Association with New Zealand
Niue lies in the South Pacific approximately 2,100 km (1,300 mi) northeast of New Zealand. It is a huge raised coral island covering an area of 259 sq km (100 sq mi). It was discovered by Captain James Cook (1728–79) in 1774 but became a British possession only in 1900. Subsequently the island was transferred to New Zealand and it became self-governing in 1974. New Zealand handles defense and foreign affairs for the island and also contributes aid to help the economy. Many of the native Polynesian population have left to work in New Zealand. Niue's chief exports include passion fruits, copra, honey, and limes. The sale of postage stamps also provides foreign currency.

NORFOLK ISLAND
Overseas Territory of Australia
Norfolk Island lies 1,600 km (1,000 mi) east of New South Wales, Australia. The island was settled in 1788 by British soldiers and convicts, and from 1825 to 1856 it was a place of misery and brutality, housing the most hardened and desperate criminals. After that, Norfolk Island became an important scene in a drama that had begun nearly 70 years earlier with the mutiny on HMS *Bounty,* when the entire community of Pitcairn—which had been the home to some of the mutineers and their descendants for 66 years—were transported there.

Each year, over 20,000 visitors come to Norfolk Island, now a thriving tourist resort, providing it with most of its income. Other revenue sources include stamps, liquor sales, and financial services. Seed from the native Norfolk pine is exported, and there is also a thriving forestry program on the island.

PITCAIRN ISLANDS
Overseas Territory of United Kingdom
In 1790 nine British sailors, together with 12 women and six men from Tahiti, arrived on Pitcairn, a small volcanic island in the Pacific Ocean midway between New Zealand and Peru. The sailors were mutineers from HMS *Bounty*. On arrival on Pitcairn the settlers burnt their ship, and for the next 18 years the island—some 5 sq km (2 sq mi) in area—became a place of violence, murder, and disease. When a party of American whalers arrived on the island in 1808 they found only one European, along with several Tahitian women and a few children. By 1856 the islands had 194 inhabitants. They were moved to Norfolk Island off the Australian coast, but 43 of them later returned to Pitcairn. Today their descendants live in Adamstown, the island's only town. They live on whatever they can grow and what they can buy from passing ships in return for stamps and curios. As well as Pitcairn, there are three other islands in the group—Henderson, Oeno, and Ducie.

TOKELAU
Overseas Territory of New Zealand
Lying about 500 km (300 mi) north of Western Samoa, the Tokelau island group appears green and lush at first sight—dense vegetation covers the three coral atolls known as Fakaofo, Nukunonu, and Atafu. Despite the abundance of coconut palms, pandanus, and other trees and shrubs, there is no fresh water on the islands—the soil is too porous to retain it. Seasonal rainfall is collected in tanks or hollowed-out coconut palm trunks.

Like many Pacific islanders, the people of Tokelau have suffered at the hands of others. A raid by Peruvian slavers in 1863 was followed by an outbreak of disease that reduced the population to about 200. In 1889 a British protectorate was established, and in 1948 the group became an island territory of New Zealand. Tokelau has a few exports, such as copra and craft items, and some revenue is derived from stamps and coins. Most people practice subsistence agriculture, and the islands also receive aid from New Zealand.

U.S. PACIFIC ISLAND WILDLIFE REFUGES (MIDWAY ISLANDS, JOHNSTON ATOLL, BAKER ISLAND, HOWLAND ISLAND, JARVIS ISLAND, KINGMAN REEF, PALMYRA ATOLL)

Unincorporated Organized Territory of the United States

These remote territories in the Pacific are managed by the Fish and Wildlife Service of the U.S. Department of Interior. They constitute the world's most widespread collection of marine and terrestrial wildlife-protected areas under a single country's jurisdiction.

Midway Islands is a coral atoll once used as a refueling stop on trans-Pacific flights. It was the scene of fierce fighting in World War II. The climate is subtropical with cool, moist winters. Today it is a National Wildlife Refuge and the site of the world's largest Laysan albatross colony. The refuge is open to the public for wildlife watching and photography. **Johnston Atoll** was mined for its guano deposits (for use in fertilizers and explosives) until the 1880s and was later used by the military. It has a tropical, generally dry climate. Johnston Island and Sand Island were designated wildlife refuges in 1926.

Baker Island was also exploited for its guano deposits. It has an equatorial climate with scant rainfall. An important site for nesting, roosting, and foraging seabirds and other marine life, it became a National Wildlife Refuge in 1974. **Howland Island** has an equatorial climate but little rain. Another important refuge for marine life, it was made a National Wildlife Refuge in 1974—as was **Jarvis Island**. Jarvis Island's climate is equatorial with little rainfall. The vegetation of scattered grasses and shrubs encourages nesting and roosting seabirds and other marine foragers.

The United States annexed **Kingman Reef** in 1922. Its sheltered lagoon served as a way station for flying boats on America–Hawaii flights in the 1930s. In 2001 the waters around the reef were designated a National Wildlife Refuge. The climate is tropical and relatively dry with northeast trade winds. **Palmyra Atoll** has a hot equatorial climate with plenty of rain, encouraging lush vegetation. It became a National Wildlife Refuge in 2001 and supports one of the largest remaining stands of Pisonia beach forest in the Pacific.

Graceful and spectacular in flight, frigatebirds are a common sight over the sea and near many of the islands in the Pacific Ocean.

WAKE ISLAND

Unincorporated Organized Territory of the United States

Wake Island lies in the western Pacific Ocean about 1,100 km (700 mi) north of Kwajalein in the Marshall Islands. It consists of three small coral islands linked by a series of causeways around a lagoon. The island receives very little rainfall, and there is no natural water source. Since 1899 it has been a U.S. territory and was

formerly used as a relay station and as a submarine and air base. The Japanese held Wake Island during World War II, from 1941–44. The island was also a refueling point for aircraft before the development of long-range jets, and it is still used as an emergency stopover point for commercial aircraft.

WALLIS AND FUTUNA
Overseas Territory of France

The French overseas territory of Wallis and Futuna comprises two small volcanic island groups lying in the southwestern Pacific Ocean to the northeast of Fiji. The humid climate coupled with rich volcanic soils typical of both island groups support abundant forest vegetation. Local government is based on the three Polynesian kingdoms of Uvéa (on the island of Wallis), Tua, and Alo (both on Futuna). More than half the total population lives on Wallis. The capital, also on Wallis, is Mata-Utu. There appears to be little appetite for independence. Subsistence farming is the main economic activity, but the islanders also export quantities of lumber and copra. The sale of fishing licences to foreign fleets (such as Japanese and Korean) also brings in revenue, as do remittances from islanders working overseas.

GLOSSARY

Words in SMALL CAPITALS refer to other entries in the Glossary.

Amerindian A member of one of the many INDIGENOUS PEOPLES of Central and South America.

Anglican A member of the PROTESTANT church—founded in England in the 16th century—including the Church of England and other churches throughout the world.

apartheid A way of organizing society to keep racial groups apart. Introduced after 1948 in South Africa by the National Party to ensure continued white political dominance, it has now been dismantled.

Buddhism A religion founded in India in the 6th and 5th centuries B.C. and based on the teachings of Gautama Siddhartha (c. 563–483 B.C.), the Buddha, or "Awakened One."

cereal A cultivated grass selectively bred to produce high yields of edible grain for consumption by humans and livestock. The most important are wheat (*Triticum*), rice (*Oryza sativa*), and maize/corn (*Zea mays*).

Christianity A religion based on the teachings of Jesus Christ and originating from JUDAISM in the 1st century A.D. Its main beliefs are found in the Bible, and it is now the world's most widespread religion, divided into a number of churches and sects, including ROMAN CATHOLICISM, PROTESTANTISM, and ORTHODOX CHURCHES.

Communism A social and economic system based on the communal ownership of property. It usually refers to the STATE-controlled social and economic systems in the former Soviet Union and Soviet bloc countries and in the People's Republic of China.

Confucianism A religion or moral code based on the teachings of the Chinese philosopher Confucius (c. 551–479 B.C.) that formed the foundations of Chinese imperial administration and ethical behavior; also followed in Korea and other east Asian countries.

constitution The fundamental statement of laws that defines the way a country is governed.

constitutional monarchy A form of government with a hereditary head of STATE or monarch and a CONSTITUTION.

democracy A form of government in which policy is made by the people (direct democracy) or on their behalf (indirect democracy). Indirect democracy usually takes the form of competition among political parties at elections.

Dependency (1) A territorial unit under the jurisdiction of another STATE but not formally annexed to it. **(2)** An unequal economic or political relationship between two states or groups of states, in which one side is dependent on and supports the other.

ethnic group A group of people sharing a social or cultural identity based on language, religion, customs and/or common descent or kinship.

EU (European Union) An alliance of European NATIONS formed to agree common policies in the areas of trade, aid, agriculture, and economics.

exports Goods or services sold to other countries.

federalism A form of CONSTITUTIONAL government in which power is shared between two levels—a central, or federal, government and a tier of provincial or STATE governments.

GDP (Gross Domestic Product) The total value of a country's annual output of goods and services with allowances made for depreciation.

Hinduism A religion originating in India in the 2nd millennium B.C. It emphasizes mystical contemplation and ascetic practices that are closely interwoven with much of Indian culture.

indigenous peoples The original inhabitants of a region.

Islam A religion based on the revelations of God to the prophet Muhammad in the 7th century A.D., as recorded in the Qu'ran. It teaches submission to the will of God and is practiced throughout the Middle East, North Africa, and parts of Southeast Asia.

Judaism A religion that developed in ancient Israel based on God's law and revelations declared to Moses on Mount Sinai.

Methodism A PROTESTANT denomination of the CHRISTIAN church based on the teachings of the English theologian John Wesley (1703–91).

monarch A form of rule where there is a hereditary head of STATE.

Muslim An adherent of ISLAM.

nation A community that believes it consists of a single people, based on historical and cultural criteria.

nation-state A STATE in which the inhabitants all belong to one NATION. Most states claim to be nation-states; in practice almost all of them include minority groups.

Native American The INDIGENOUS PEOPLES of North America.

official language The language used by governments, schools, courts, and other official institutions in countries where the population has no single common mother tongue.

one-party state A political system in which there is no competition to the government party at elections, as in COMMUNIST and military regimes.

parliamentary democracy A political system in which the legislature (Parliament) is elected by all the adult members of the population and the government is formed by the party that commands a majority in the Parliament.

Protestant Term describing CHRISTIAN denominations that share a common rejection of the authority of the pope as head of the church, and of many ROMAN CATHOLIC practices.

Roman Catholic The largest of the CHRISTIAN churches, headed by the pope in Rome. It traces its origin and authority to St. Peter, one of the disciples of Jesus Christ and the first bishop of Rome. There are believers on all continents.

Shi'ite Muslim A member of the smaller of the two main divisions of ISLAM. Followers recognize Muhammad's son-in-law, Ali, and his descendants, the imams (prayer leaders), as his true successors and legitimate leaders of Islam.

state The primary political unit of the modern world, usually defined by its possession of sovereignty over a territory and its people.

subtropical The climatic zone between the TROPICS and TEMPERATE zones. There are marked seasonal changes of temperature but it is never very cold.

Sunni Muslim A member of the larger of the two main divisions of ISLAM. Its members recognize the Caliphs as the successors to Muhammad and follow the *sunna*, or way of the prophet, as recorded in the *hadithw*, the teachings of Muhammad.

temperate climate Any one of the climatic zones in mid-latitudes, with a mild climate. They cover areas between the warm TROPICS and cold polar regions.

tropics (tropical) The area between the Tropic of Cancer (23°30'N) and the Tropic of Capricorn (23°30'S), marking the lines of latitude farthest from the equator where the Sun is still found directly overhead at midday in midsummer.

FURTHER REFERENCES

General Reference Books

Allen, J. L., *Student Atlas of World Geography*, McGraw-Hill, Columbus, OH, 2004.

Atlas of World Geography, Rand McNally, Chicago, IL, 2005.

Baines, J. D., Egan, V., and G. Bateman, *The Encyclopedia of World Geography: A Country by Country Guide*, Thunder Bay, San Diego, CA, 2003.

de Blij, H. J., and P. O. Muller, *Concepts and Regions in Geography*, John Wiley & Sons, New York, 2004.

Muller, P. O., and E. Muller-Hames, *Geography, Study Guide: Realms, Regions, and Concepts*, John Wiley & Sons, New York, 2005.

Oxford Atlas of the World, Oxford University Press, New York, 2003.

Parsons, J. (ed.), *Geography of the World*, DK Children, London and New York, 2006.

Peoples of the World: Their Cultures, Traditions, and Ways of Life, National Geographic, Washington, DC, 2001.

Pulsipher, L. M., *World Regional Geography: Global Patterns, Local Lives*, W. H. Freeman, New York, 2005.

Warf, B. (ed.), *Encyclopedia of Human Geography*, Sage Publications, London and New York, 2006.

Specific to this volume

Blouet, B. W., and O. M. Blouet, *Latin America and the Caribbean: A Systematic and Regional Survey*, John Wiley & Sons, New York, 2005.

Clawson, D. L., *Latin America and the Caribbean*, McGraw Hill Science, New York, 2005.

De Roy, T., and M. Jones, *New Zealand: A Natural History*, Firefly Books, Buffalo, NY, 2006.

Howe, K. R., *Nature, Culture and History: The Knowing of Oceania*, University of Hawaii Press, Honolulu, 2001.

Kent, R. B., *Latin America: Regions and People*, The Guilford Press, New York, 2006.

Place, S. E. (ed.), *Tropical Rainforest: Latin American Nature and Society in Transition* (Jaguar Books on Latin America, No. 2), Scholarly Resources, Wilmington, DE, 2001.

Powell, J. M., *An Historical Geography of Modern Australia*, Cambridge University Press, Cambridge, UK, 2004.

Robinson, G. M., Loughran, R. J., and P. Tranter, *Australia and New Zealand: Economy, Society and Environment*, Edward Arnold, London, 2000.

Stonehouse, B., *The Last Continent: Discovering Antarctica*, Odyssey, Hong Kong, 2000.

Sumner, R. (ed.), *World Geography: South and Central America*, Oxford University Press, New York, 2007.

Sumner, R., and R. K. Rasmussen (eds.), *World Geography: Antarctica, Australia, and the Pacific*, Salem Press, Pasadena, CA, 2001.

Troy, P. N., *Australian Cities: Issues, Strategies and Policies for Urban Australia in the 1990s*, Cambridge University Press, Cambridge, UK, 1999.

Wiarda, H. J., *The Soul of Latin America: The Cultural and Political Tradition*, Yale University Press, New Haven, CT, 2003.

General Web Sites

www.ethnologue.com
A comprehensive guide to all the languages of the world.

www.factmonster.com/ipka/A0770414.html
Geography facts and figures for kids.

www.geographic.org
Information on geography for students, teachers, parents, and children.

www.odci.gov/cia/publications/factbook/index.html
Central Intelligence Agency factbook of country profiles.

ww.panda.org
World Wide Fund for Nature (WWF).

www.peoplegroups.org/default.aspx
Listing and information on major ethnic groups around the world.

www.worldatlas.com
A world atlas of facts, flags, and maps.

INDEX